The Vegetarian's Guide to Eating Meat

MARISSA LANDRIGAN

The Vegetarian's Guide to Eating Meat

A Young Woman's Search for Ethical Food

GREYSTONE BOOKS

Vancouver/Berkeley

Greystone Books Ltd.
www.greystonebooks.com

Cataloguing data available from Library and Archives Canada
ISBN 978-1-77164-274-3 (pbk.)
ISBN 978-1-77164-275-0 (epub)

Editing by Jennifer Croll
Copyediting by Shirarose Wilensky
Proofreading by Alison Strobel
Cover and text design by Nayeli Jimenez
Illustrations by Nayeli Jimenez
Printed and bound in Canada on ancient-forest-friendly paper by Friesens

We gratefully acknowledge the support of the Canada Council for
the Arts, the British Columbia Arts Council, the Province of British Columbia
through the Book Publishing Tax Credit, and the Government of
Canada for our publishing activities.

Canadä

BRITISH COLUMBIA   BRITISH COLUMBIA ARTS COUNCIL
An agency of the Province of British Columbia

Canada Council   Conseil des arts
for the Arts   du Canada

Contents

Chapter One

Head Cheese

I **WAS STANDING IN** knee-high rubber boots, watching blood pool in translucent puddles, then drift slowly towards the drains in the center of the sloped concrete floor. My long hair was bunched up under a plastic shower cap, pulled down nearly over my eyebrows and around my ears. I wasn't talking much, because it was noisy in there: the hum and whirr of an electric meat saw cutting through flesh, the metallic lurch of a pulley hoisting thousand-pound bodies up to the rafters, the hole-punch ricochet of a bolt gun, and the resultant crumpling collapse. I was just watching, as the staff of six worked the Wednesday morning slaughter line at Black Earth Meats in Black Earth, Wisconsin. And I was staring at the skinned head of a steer.

The lower half of the steer's jaw had been removed and the thick tongue cut out, tossed heavily onto a nearby metal cart for later packaging, and the entire head had been skinned. Not scalded clean—the eyeballs and all the muscle were still intact—but the hide had been pulled gently backwards over itself, to reveal the maze of tendon and sinew just below the surface. The head hung on a butcher hook not six feet from me, the sharp tongs of the hook punching up into what was once the roof of the steer's mouth. The head was suspended there, half-removed mouth gaping, metal curves protruding from below its teeth like fangs. The eyeballs bulged without lids to protect them, staring out at me, looking wild and scared and confused.

I was completely fascinated by that head. I could not stop staring at it, at the crazy sideways eyes, the webbing of red muscles crossing back and forth over themselves like gauze, a bandage wrapped around the white skull. I thought it was beautiful, to see the inner life of a body exposed that way, to learn the under-skin mysteries of my food. But then, while I was staring this intently, the cheek of the dead steer twitched.

I jumped a little, shaking in those borrowed rubber boots, and watched as one of the muscles in the steer's cheek pulsed and flinched again and again, involuntary spasms, convulsing the entire skull, a synapse quake. In half a beat, I regained my composure. I'd read enough to know that this was not an indication that the steer was still alive. *All its skin is gone,* I reminded myself, *its head is fully severed.* Sometimes, after death, reflexive muscle spasms will occur. They mean nothing.

I knew all this, which is why I could go on staring, as the exposed muscles of the steer's skull continued twitching and dancing, its feral eyes still casting out at me blindly, in death, perpetually half-eating the tongs of a meat hook. Although my mouth hung open slightly with wild captivation, I could say later, when recounting this story, that the skinned head of the steer provoked in me no visceral or emotional response. I remained curious, not disgusted.

I WATCHED THE exquisite ballet of the slaughter emerge. I watched as the man with the moustache and the electric knife worked the hide loose from the steer's body, from the hind legs and haunches, from the gut and back. Silent and quick, he whirred the flesh loose, then clipped the steer's hind legs into a massive pulley system, which let out a groaning squeal and strained to lift the dead steer up, up. Two more men in aprons attached what looked like a giant set of tongs to each of the loose flaps of skin. Pulley and tongs yanked at the steer, pulling in opposition, peeling the hide back off the dead body. White fascia tissue clung intently to the inside of the skin. The tail pulled nearly to the floor with resistance, then sprang back up and whacked the dead steer's stomach. The steer hung, inverted and skinned, after only five minutes.

I continued to watch, intent on discovery. I learned that a saw durable enough to cut a steer in half, straight down through its bones, existed. In a breathtaking whirl of blades and bones and blood, the rest of the crew descended on the body, to create from a whole dead steer a pile of component parts: two long slabs of side body for processing into butcher cuts; hooves and horns and hard parts for grinding; liver and heart and tongue for offal; skinned skull on a meat hook, to be boiled later for head cheese.

BUT THE THING I learned that day in the slaughterhouse, that I learned by being quieter than I ever thought I could be, the thing that stayed with me the longest, was what it looked like when a steer was struck brain-dead by a bolt gun. I learned that nobody was looking at me, so it was okay if I jumped when the gun went off, at the enormous noise of metal shooting through skull. I learned deep in my bones the sensation of collapse, the thump of the body to the floor.

As I felt the twinge in my jaw from grinding my teeth together, I learned that the body has its own dance of death, that the body doesn't lie still. The animal thrashed. Its legs, wild with firing synapses, kicked desperately, frantically, kicked like the animal was still in there, kicked as if an electric pulse was running through its muscles, kick as if it was trying to stand up.

AS I STOOD in the slaughterhouse that day, I sensed I was being taught something. I knew I couldn't, not for one second, take my eyes off the skinned head of the steer. There was a secret for me there, under the skin. I didn't yet know what it was—for now, there were only questions. Only one question, really, a constant whirring through my mind, as I stared at the strange dancing skinned head of the steer: *How the hell did I get here?*

How did this happen? What was this tiny weird girl with the disposable shower cap doing there, on a pleasantly cool early morning in May, in the fuzzy green hills of southwest Wisconsin, standing in a puddle of blood, watching a truck full of cattle get killed?

Chapter Two

Al Dente

IT NEVER OCCURRED to me, growing up, that a wooden folding rack might actually be used for drying clothes—because in my house, we used it to dry pasta. We were an Italian-American home, a ravioli-every-Christmas-Eve home, the kind of home where everyone was present for family dinners on weeknights and kids spent their Saturdays making wine, ankle-deep in the stomping barrels of great-grandparents' backyards. The kind of home that I now know wasn't that common in 1980s suburban America.

My great-great-grandparents came by boat from Italy, and even four generations later, although only my mother was Italian and my father was full Irish, at the heart of my childhood home my parents built an Italian kitchen—a heritage-rich enclave—in the middle of suburban New Hampshire, where every couple of months my entire family would converge to make fresh pasta together. Although we tried to make our pasta as authentic as possible, this wasn't Italy—it was Merrimack, a town with neither a butcher shop nor a farmers market—so, in true suburban fashion, we all piled into our boxy maroon Chrysler minivan and drove to Costco to get flour, butter, and eggs, in bulk.

Although Merrimack did have a slight rural bent, this was more a product of its age than of an actual lingering agricultural industry. By the time we moved there, it was just a typical American suburb, where my mother and I spent most of my childhood Saturdays on cold metal bleachers watching my sisters play soccer, and my father, clipboard in hand, coached from the sidelines. The town's primary employers were Fidelity Investments financial services provider; BAE Systems defense, security, and aerospace company; Brookstone retail stores; and Anheuser-Busch brewery, whose Budweiser Clydesdales marched every summer in our Fourth of July parade—an all-American gathering, which always smelled of sweet barbequed meat tended to by pot-bellied, white-haired men. There were sparklers and stars, children with tangled hair and sticky fingers.

Run-down, but not decrepit, our town was a mix of undertended relics of history amid half-empty plazas and strip malls. It was an old village with cemeteries whose graves dated back to the eighteenth century, including one we'd often bike to in the summers to do grave rubbings on pieces of wax paper. There were signs denoting the birthplace of great historical figures, such as Matthew Thornton, Merrimack resident and signer of the Declaration of Independence, but there were also dingy laundromats, neglected discount stores, and overcrowded schools.

As far as meals were concerned, we rarely ordered takeout or went out to dinner as a family in our town, but when we did, we went to a restaurant called the Common Man, a New England franchise built into a house, complete with attic bar and stone fireplaces. On the way there, I remember driving past a dilapidated bowling alley, one small Mexican restaurant, and three greasy Chinese joints.

In my memory, all the places in between rise before me like an overgrown forest, even though much of those swathes of pine trees have disappeared now. There were rolling hills and dense foliage that gave me the distinct impression of always being underneath something. Whenever I looked to the sky, there were leaves in the way. Although the town is larger than a village now, and the population is mostly middle class, those hills and forests, like the historical markers, were a reminder of the logging industry around which New Hampshire was industrialized. The story of Merrimack is told in red flannel and maple syrup, a story of long winters and hard-fought wars.

MY OWN STORY began inside a gray, distinctly New England house on a sleepy corner lot, or, more specifically, in a noisy, crowded kitchen with a peel-and-stick laminate floor painted to look like red brick. From my vantage point, hiding beneath a dark-stained behemoth of a kitchen table, that faux brick floor, always covered in stumbling, busy feet, stretched out like a crowded market in the midst of my family's own small civilization.

The kitchen was divided in half by an island that protruded from one wall, a heavy wooden arm separating the dining half of the room from an area with three walls stuffed full of dark wood cabinets, white laminate countertops, and dated appliances. I have no idea how all our pots and pans were crammed into such a small space. And it's an even bigger mystery how my mother, father, sisters, and grandparents all fit, too, but pasta making was group work, daylong work, and it required all hands.

Because I was shy, I'd hide underneath the enormous table my parents had been given as a wedding present whenever the kitchen became too loud. In all of our houses—ours, my grandparents', my great-grandparents'—there was a table in the kitchen, even when there was a separate formal dining room, even when we couldn't all fit around it. And I would crawl beneath the table and barricade myself from the racket and the clamor, piling books around me and peering out at the frenzied dance from beneath the hem of the tablecloth. Behind the protective shield of my coke-bottle glasses, I watched these days of my childhood unfold as rituals, a series of elaborate steps constructed to make all the moving parts work as a whole.

In preparation for the pasta-making ceremony, my big Irish dad would wrestle open the drying rack in the corner. With the body of a bear, legs and arms so thick I couldn't wrap both hands around them and touch my fingertips, pale Irish skin, freckles, and my same ice-blue eyes, he was an intimidating figure, at least according to more than one boyfriend whose hands he gripped perhaps just a little too tightly. In our kitchen, it was his job to create order. He was the dad who brought a Fodor's guidebook on every family vacation, who made chore charts that rotated weekly based on birth order, but he was not much of a cook. So when we made pasta, it was my father who started early, who laid out all the equipment in stages: drying rack in the corner by the back door, pasta machine on the edge of the counter, rolling pin and flour on the opposite side of the kitchen, waiting for the dough.

When we weren't eating, I would sit beside my father at that enormous kitchen table, doing my math homework. I was bookish, a word person—still am. I liked flowery language. Math was a constant struggle, the bane of my honor-roll existence. It wasn't that I didn't like math, or that I couldn't see the beauty of geometry and imaginary numbers—it was that beauty didn't get the equation solved. As a math major in college, my father's interest in numbers was an obsession. He built himself a lifelong career in Internet technology sales and marketing from the ground up with his intuitive understanding of supply and demand. My father loved helping me with my math homework, took pride in trying to engender in his eldest daughter a fascination with the shape of the world as he saw it. We would spend hours together, huddled over a textbook, his big finger pointing, guiding me across a page: *So, if you divide both sides of the equation by (abc) then you can isolate x...*

This is why it was his job to establish the order of pasta making, and once he did, my mother and Nana, my grandmother, would begin to work the chewy-tough spaghetti dough into long flat ribbons, wide as a palm and a quarter-inch thick. My mother would hunch over the counter, brushing from her eyes the wild, curly hair she could only tame by pinning the sides back with plastic combs in tortoiseshell and black. With brown eyes and olive skin, she looked the part of a Mediterranean matriarch. Her beauty routine, like her cooking, was meticulous. The bathroom closet was always packed full of creams, lotions, powders, and makeup. She still paints her nails every weekend and wears the same pattern of rings every day, on the same fingers: her diamond engagement ring and gold wedding band in the traditional location, plus a thin band of jade on her right-hand ring finger.

Although we learned to make pasta from my great-grandmother, my mother was always the center of our household. She has a master's degree and a long impressive career, but she will tell you that her greatest achievement in life is her family, and that responsibility was both heartwarming and overwhelming. My sisters and I would often get the overly dramatic Catholic-mom guilt if we wanted to spend a Saturday night at a friend's place. *You don't want to spend time with us, with your family?* She emphasized the "with your family" part, giving it a gravity that seemed to imply the family might not be there when you got back. Traditions mattered deeply to her. Every Christmas Eve, after evening mass, after ravioli dinner at my grandparents' house; after she had prepared the morning's two quiches, raspberry coffee cake, and ham frittata; after the coffeemaker was readied—even if all this took until midnight—we were still expected to gather around the television to watch the silent animated film *The Snowman.* Traditions, to my mother, were a road map to your past, how you remembered, ritualized, who you were as a unit. *Because this is what we've always done.*

My mother could exude warmth and engender fear in equal parts. My childhood friends knew she would yell at them for breaking house rules, but when a hungry teenage boy showed up to work on a science project or play guitar with me in the backyard, my mother was always there, offering a "snack," like leftover chicken drumsticks or homemade pepper and onion pizza. She was a force, a presence. As a public school teacher, her voice echoed throughout the house, from one story up and a hallway down, when she yelled for help moving a piece of furniture, or to tell my sisters and me she could hear us fighting. She talked with her mouth full and she interrupted. She had only one speed, and it was go.

I assume her ability to direct a flock of eighth graders to sing and dance on cue for the school's annual play had something to do with why she didn't mind the chaos of a crowded kitchen, the clutter and noise that sent me beneath the table. She was in her element there, surrounded by family, shouting over everyone, her palms gripping a wooden rolling pin, her brown arms flexing softly as she bore down on the dough.

While Mom and Nana worked the dough, Meaghan and Caitlin, my all-Italian sisters, with their rich brown hair and liquid eyes, would scatter around the kitchen like chattering monkeys, pretending to help, mischievously throwing handfuls of flour against the counter where it would explode in small dusty clouds. Both dark skinned with glasses and curly hair, my sisters, practically twins, operated as a unit. When the family gathered around old photo albums and flipped through the mid- to late-1980s, even my mother had to pull out a print and look at the year or caption on the back to figure out which of her younger two she was looking at. They were a neat line from my mother, clearly her daughters in both physical appearance and temperament. I was the crooked line.

Although I am the eldest, we are all the same age apart— each just twenty months from the next—so age alone doesn't explain why they ended up so similar and I so different. Meaghan and Caitlin were tough in body and light in spirit, in contrast to my physical frailty and fascination with darkness. Never much interested in intellectual pursuits, they both loved spicy food, salsa dancing, and shouting. They always shared a unique bond of dance routines and soccer practices and nicknames. While my family was in the early stages of making pasta dough, they never had the patience to stand still long enough to help. They'd hold contests to see who could scramble up the inside of the kitchen doorframe faster, their backs against one side of the frame, their bare monkey feet against the other, powering their tiny bodies up to the ceiling. As for me, I waited. I had only one job, and it came later in the process.

It was Gampi, my grandfather, who manhandled the pasta machine, a clunky metal contraption with rolling plates and munching teeth. The edge of the counter was chipped slightly from the vice grip of the machine, which my grandfather tightened with his gnarled fingers. By the time Mom and Nana had the dough rolled flat enough, Gampi was ready. The two women gingerly carried the dough over to their father, husband, together, palms crossed beneath each other at the sagging center. They lifted it vertically and guided one swaying end gently into the patient metal rollers of the pasta machine. Gampi began turning the hand crank—nothing automated here—and the dough was pulled down into the machine. They ran the floured sheets through the machine three or four times, each pass thinning the dough to nearly tissue-paper consistency, too thin for human hands or clunky rolling pins to achieve. The dough grew even longer in their hands, its excessive thickness stretched and redistributed as length, until Mom called me over to drape the yard-long cool cloth of dough over my pale freckled arms.

Gampi lifted and unfolded the machine from itself, raising the slicing attachment into its place over the edge of the counter. These were the crucial moments that moved so slowly, requiring full cooperation and attention. I had to feed the dough back towards the machine at just the right pace. Too fast and the pasta bunched up on itself, and the entire flattening process had to be repeated. Not fast enough, and the dough pulled apart, a slow yanking pressure until it snapped like popped bubblegum. Mom and Nana guided the dough up and over, down into the machine at the perfect angle, making sure never to let it brush up against the edge of the machine where it would snag and tear. And Gampi turned the crank quickly, more quickly than you would think, pumping it insistently, until magically, out of the bottom of the machine grew dancing sprouts of spaghetti like freshly cut wheat, into my father's waiting hands.

Dad gathered the pasta like yarn, spread between his two palms so that the damp dough wouldn't stick back onto itself. He backed slowly, slowly away from the machine, bent at the waist, until the dough was just about to pass clean through. My mother came around to catch the other end, and I watched, having again retreated beneath the table, as my parents took the sweeping strands of pasta, together, towards the drying rack. Meaghan and Caitlin would leap to attention, pretending to carry the pasta too, tiny brown hands reaching up underneath the sagging blanket, inches above their palms. My parents never shooed them away. When the pasta was resting safely against the drying rack, everyone exhaled slightly. One batch down.

In all this work emerged an extended dance, all of us bowing and swaying around each other, backs pressed against walls to avoid collision, sliding from one spot to the next with broken pieces in our hands, the disparate parts that would eventually become a meal. Our cooking was a collective effort that blended the Irish in my father and the freckles on my skin into the Italian of the rest, across centuries and state lines and homelands, our family a single unit in the pursuit of the perfect pasta. There is no such thing as too crowded a kitchen.

LATER, WHEN WE cooked our new creation in steaming copper-bottomed pots, the pasta rolling in the boiling water, Gampi taught his granddaughters how to test its doneness, how to tell when the pasta had reached al dente perfection. He dipped a clawed wooden spoon into the pot and gathered a few wet strands into his callused palms, letting them drip dry over the sink, and then flung them against the kitchen wall. Nana scolded, but Gampi knew my mother would never tell him to stop. From where she stood in the kitchen corner, looking on fondly, I could see how her memory flooded with these lessons from her own childhood. If the pasta sticks, clinging to the white paint, not sliding more than a millimeter down the wall's smooth surface, then it's ready to eat.

Hanging on the kitchen wall, above the large table, was a framed print of Norman Rockwell's *Freedom from Want*, wherein an elderly matriarch places a giant turkey onto a crowded white-clothed table. This was the image I saw whenever we ate together, and it seemed perfectly familiar to me: the commotion of elbows knocking into each other, the shouts to pass the mashed potatoes or gravy, the slightly outdated formality of the wallpapered walls and crystal dishes. Dinners, for my family, were a raucous, celebratory affair. Food was tradition. Food was connection. Food was family.

I carried the lessons of this kitchen with me, embedded in memory, even as I grew up and moved away, missed family dinners and, later, skipped the meatballs. I was taught that if you worked hard, and worked together, food was the great reward. Now, years removed from my childhood kitchen, the shape of each family member blurs slightly in my memory, allowing me to see the patterns rather than just the people, the choreography, the larger ritual being enacted. I learned that cooking was our way of communicating with each other, and that in the spinning around and between each other, we were saying, *Be careful, I'm right here, I love you.*

WHEN I WAS about five years old, there was a giant gathering at my great-grandparents' house in Dedham, Massachusetts. This was the small city my great-great-grandparents, Nona and Papa, picked when they arrived from Italy by boat, the town in which my grandfather and mother both grew up, a little less than fifteen miles outside of Boston. We visited Dedham often when I was a girl, and this time, we were there for a sort of family reunion, though I didn't know most of my mother's extended family well. Someone—probably my grandfather—had wrapped a long white banner of dot-matrix printer paper around the house: a family tree. A line stretched down its center, names branching off from that line written neatly with colored markers in dark green, blue, red. I could barely even pronounce some of those long and flowing names, with clicks and extended vowels and heavy second-syllable articulation: Corsini, Squillante, Berlusconi, Salvaimo. First names like the grapevines lacing around their brittle bushes: Margherita, Paulina, Oresti, Antoni. And way down towards the right side of the house, in the present day, Marissa.

In need of a break from the noise, I remember standing against the side of the house in my pink floral dress, looking back and forth between the strangers scattered across the green summer lawn and the road map of names lining the house, trying to figure out how these people belonged on this map, and how they were my family.

I had escaped the legions of aunts, big lumbering women, all of whom looked exactly like Nona, slightly hunched and limping with ulcers here and there, the flaps of fat on their upper arms waving as they charged towards me. The aunts always wore pantyhose, even then, in the middle of a New England July, but they never hesitated to take off their shoes. Their brown, toughened fingers, knotted like the bark of Papa's apple trees, tangled in my thick blonde hair and laced around my wrist in amazement at how much of the bone they could see. I was dragged to the banquet table of fat, round meatballs and tiny chicken and pork tortellini three times after I ate of my own will, with stops along the way for the aunts, their red dresses billowing out like tents, to show the uncles how my mother had not been feeding me.

Tomato sauce splattered lightly across the cream collar of my dress, I retreated behind the corner of the tidy house. The lawn rolled out easily into the neighbors' lawn, with no fences to separate them other than Papa's rows of tomato plants and grapevines and apple trees. The neighboring houses were owned by cousins, children, old friends who shared ocean voyages, Saturdays at the salon, childbirth and child-rearing, grape crushing, garden planting, and wide, stretched-out knee-high stockings. I was young and pale and blonde, distanced from their bulging bodies and thick accents by generations and my suburban American culture. My mother and sisters fit; their appearances matched the second- and third-generation women in that backyard, and so did their personalities. Meaghan and Caitlin happily danced in the attentions of these distant relatives, while I retreated.

My parents had a videotape of the day, just an hour or so of panning footage. I don't remember who was filming or who narrated—probably my mother's brother, Paul, the aspiring artist of the family. But I do remember watching the video once as a family, many years later, laughing and pointing at our younger selves, at how much we'd changed. Since I'd hidden for most of the day from the loud, brash voices of my extended family, I only made one appearance on the tape. The cameraman was speaking to Papa, who sat on a folding chair in the backyard, his banjo slung across his lap. I crept into the right corner of the camera's frame, my hair-sprayed bangs framing big glasses. I looked deeply concerned, my eyes wide and mouth pinched. I glanced at Papa, opened my mouth as if to speak, then darted my head up and to the sides, sharply, like a chicken, and wandered offscreen.

NO ONE WHO meets me in person, who sees my auburn hair, lily-white skin, ice-blue eyes, and rampant freckles, believes that I am at all Italian. When I was six years old, waiting with my mother in the lobby of the studio where my sisters took tap-jazz class, I heard for the first time what would be the defining joke of my childhood. My mother introduced me to another mom, who commented that she couldn't believe how different we looked from each other. My mother smiled, put her arm around my shoulder, waist-high to her and said, "Yup, that's Marissa—the milkman's daughter." Although I was puzzled at the time—we didn't even have a milkman—I understood pretty quickly that I did not fit into this crowd of authentic Italian women.

Italian women cook. This is what we do.

In my earliest kitchen memories, I'm peering out from beneath the small round oak table in Nona's kitchen in Dedham. Nona's kitchen was even smaller than ours, and was always full—with the women of my family, but also with the Italian friends and neighbors. The kitchen steamed with the humid scents of boiling water and aging cheese, the stinging pinch of garlic and tomatoes sticking in their tousled hair. These women always sounded like they were yelling—mostly in English, with the occasional ingredient named in Italian—but this was just their natural volume. Thick hands dug deep into bowls of ground beef. Dots and smudges of white flour stuck against sweaty olive forearms and in strong black eyebrows. A unit. A pack. *Because this is what we've always done.*

Nona, limping and white-haired, could barely manage a flight of stairs, but she could command a room with the clang of a ladle against a pot. My mother managed to work a full-time job, raise three children within three years of each other in age, get her master's in education part time in the evenings, and have a hot meal on the table every night. You better believe we sat still, bowed our heads, and gave thanks. Nobody was allowed to skip family dinner. This was the power of food. And it was always women, with the occasional exception of a communal cooking fest or a summer evening cookout, who made the food.

But not me. Worse than my bookish, quiet nature, worse than my skinny hips, the thing that most distinguished me from the loud, vibrant, powerful women of my family was my complete lack of abilities in the kitchen. I was a terrible cook. My mind was too everywhere-all-the-time, too chaotic and stormy to focus on any one thing, whether walking in a straight line or following a recipe. I bumped into doors and walls, smacked myself in the face with dancing, expressive hands, dropped and tripped over things constantly. And this clumsiness escalated to dangerous levels within the confines of the kitchen.

I'm the one who, while carrying a fresh batch of pasta across the kitchen, tripped over an untied shoelace and dropped a whole wet pile to the floor. When I was a teenager, my mother left me alone to reheat leftovers for my own dinner because everyone else had basketball practice or parent-teacher conferences, and I ended the night standing on a kitchen stool, crying, scrubbing mashed potatoes off the ceiling. One high school afternoon, a friend invited me to her house for lunch and asked me, while she ran to the bathroom, to watch the hot dogs she had set to sizzle in a skillet. She returned to find me, mouth twisted in worry, staring intently at the charred, black meat. At age ten, I made cookie dough so rubbery that when my six-year-old sister tried a bite from the bowl, the tough sugary mass stuck so hard against her baby canine it pulled clear of the gum. She ran crying from the kitchen to my mother, while I stood, guiltily, holding a bloody, unbaked cookie in my hand.

I don't remember any single moment of humiliation, any one action that caused my mother to point, furious, and ban me from the kitchen. I just know I was never really invited—nor did I ever really want to be. I preferred to stand just outside, to hide beneath the table, to watch, sensing there was something that set me apart. Food was the bedrock of my family, the means of expression, and the solid foundation on which all of our connection was built. But I wasn't an Italian goddess in the kitchen, so I had to be something else.

WHEN I WAS young, I attributed most of the difference between my mother and sisters and me to body type. Both my sisters have been taller than me since adolescence, and both had round, full bodies, the bodies of *women*, bodies described as curvy or generous or soft. I always assumed it was the self-possession that came with an adult female body that made them boisterous, more playful and extroverted than me. They knew something about being a woman, something that made them want to curl their hair and wear makeup, something I was missing. I aligned my failures in the kitchen with a general disdain for anything I deemed too girly.

Once every few months, to indulge their taste for the spicy, my mother and sisters would have what they called "girls' night out." They would dress up, taking the excuse to use their curling irons, to wear heels and eyeliner, and head out on the town for a more international approach to fine dining, and to catch a romantic comedy at the theater by the mall.

I stayed home with my father, relieved to have narrowly avoided getting roped into what I thought of then as far too girly a night. We'd order a couple of pizzas, wasting none of our time in the kitchen, and he'd let me watch him watch sports on ESPN while I ate off a paper plate on the pale lavender carpet of the living room floor. Surrounded by floral furniture and light periwinkle walls dotted with collages of family photographs, and framed art class creations from us girls, I made my first little rebellions against the culture of womanhood, a culture that seemed to me based mostly on the proper applications for lip gloss, or burning the edges of your forehead on various hair-heating devices, and a far too adventurous approach to food.

Although my father and grandfather participated in our family's communal cooking sessions, by and large, my family followed more traditional gender roles, with stay-at-home moms doing most of the food preparation and working dads earning money outside the house. But more important, to me, was that my father and I shared a pickiness in our food tastes. We both ate spaghetti and meatballs but eschewed the spicier offerings like sausages or less-Americanized choices like tiramisu and cannoli.

My father sat on the couch, opposite the television, while I sat cross-legged on the floor by the coffee table. He'd drink a Sam Adams straight from the bottle while we watched the

Celtics rattle the backboards at the Garden, him leaping up with each basket made. We'd laugh as I imitated him, launching myself into the air, coming down on one knee, and pumping my elbow backwards, yelling, "Yeah, baby!"

These nights with my father were my private victories. A dividing line emerged in my brain, one I struggle even now to articulate, because the truth is, it was pretty arbitrary. All I knew at the time was that, somehow, I shared more in common with him than either of my sisters, despite the fact that they actually played on the basketball and soccer teams he coached. I must have sensed that I was missing out on something, watching my sisters from a distance as they learned to use chopsticks and hair straighteners, wrinkling my nose at the mysterious cardboard containers they brought home, bottoms spotted with grease from thick yogurt sauces, or round aluminum plates with crumpled edges full of seaweed rolls and thin strips of ginger. I decided I didn't want to learn *that* way to be a woman. I know now these were little more than introvert rumblings: I preferred staying in to going out, and because my father did too, I thought that made me less of a girly girl. This was my idea, at the time, of feminism, of political identity: I began to define myself by what I chose not to do—ignoring any kind of beauty regimen, and making a statement with what I refused to eat.

MY PARENTS STILL live in that house, and have for more than twenty years. It underwent constant change while I was growing up, each of the rooms stripped to the studs and rebuilt at least once in my lifetime. But I still remember my solitary moments there, the moments that set me apart—beneath the kitchen table, silent in the crowd of a family meal, on the living room floor with a slice of pizza. I remember ice-skating with books in the living room, a hardcover under each foot allowing me to glide across the lavender carpet.

I don't remember the moment I knew I would move far away from there.

The year I finished high school, my parents took us to Europe for nearly three weeks, and one morning, our last in London, I volunteered to run down the street from our rented flat to get breakfast from the corner market while my sisters slept in and took showers. I don't remember what I bought. But I remember so clearly the rush I got from walking through the city, even just a few blocks, on my own. Although I'd often been to Boston, just an hour south of my hometown, I'd always been with friends or family, and the same applied anytime I had ventured outside our suburb. As far as I could recall, this was my first time alone in a city, on the cusp of eighteen and leaving for college, and I saw my life as one big possibility. I could picture a future, an adulthood, here, in a way I never could imagine in Merrimack.

I imagined mornings, wrapped in a trench coat and trendy scarf, where I'd take the subway to my job, something smart and creative, like bookstore owner or editor at a boutique publishing house. I'd know my local shop owners and buy wine and cheese for park picnics on the weekends. I'd be the kind of person who always kept fresh hydrangeas in her house. Although it was late June, the London breeze whipped my newly short hair around my ears, which were buzzing with the certainty that my future would begin in a city.

I was a quiet, clumsy girl surrounded by brassy, confident women who were comfortable in heels or in the kitchen. People who met my family for the first time assumed I was adopted. Rather than be left out, branded the too-awkward tomboy, I chose a different identity for myself. Somehow, food and domesticity became all muddled; without even realizing it, I'd conflated cooking with regressive gender roles. My father was my closest physical analog in the family, so I took my first steps in self-identity towards him, away from the rituals of our shared kitchen, away from femininity. Food became my mutiny.

Chapter Three

Meet Your Meat

BY THE TIME I turned eighteen, I was ready to go, ready for something bigger than Merrimack. Although I'd never lived anywhere else, the thought of staying in New Hampshire for college never appealed to me: I was hungry for something new, and I found that at Ithaca College.

Ithaca is a vibrant place, an idyllic campus in New York's Finger Lakes region, four hours removed from the bustle of Manhattan, set atop a hill overlooking a swirling city of brilliant academics, hungry young entrepreneurs, and Burning Man enthusiasts. Within fifteen minutes, I could walk across campus: pristine green quads full of barefoot young men playing Hacky Sack and strumming Dave Matthews songs on their guitars. Originally founded as a music conservatory and now with a strong reputation in journalism, the college had a population that was both intelligent and engaged: theater majors alongside communications majors with minors in business or political science.

But it was the city below that I loved: the pedestrians-only Commons full of Thai restaurants, divey sports bars, and head shops; the Mexican restaurant painted turquoise and orange; Moosewood Restaurant, tucked in a basement-level spot inside a mall, its window glowing yellow onto the street outside. Walking along the Commons, I could forget the freezing sting of the Finger Lakes wind. This was a place of energy, a place I felt a young girl could come alive. Sometimes, I just drove around the city, getting lost on purpose on the winding side streets, finding my way up the other hill to Cornell's college town neighborhood, to a stone tower I'd never seen before, or a massive waterfall. Ithaca was a city of constant surprises: a church flying a gay pride flag, a house painted purple.

By the beginning of my second year at Ithaca, I'd embraced how different I'd become from my family, forced the wedge further, and had fully adopted the part of the neophyte radical. Having just recently been dumped by the first boy I fell in love with, I'd chopped my hair off and pierced my lip, and I was skipping class fairly regularly to spend as much time as possible with my two closest friends, Caity and Meghan. They were endlessly fascinating. Caity: a film and photography major who'd grown up in a brownstone in Yonkers, with porcelain skin and a strong Greek nose, her nearly black hair cropped short and straight around her stunning face. Meghan: a sociology major fixated on Mexican culture, quickly developing her now-fluent Spanish, with curly hair and always a soft, blissful smile while dancing. Both introduced me to exciting new music: the punk-pop of Saves the Day, the hard thrashing of Converge, the upbeat salsa of Celia Cruz.

I was a young activist who hadn't quite figured out yet what that meant, but I knew I had a big heart that seemed to be splitting with all the suffering I was learning existed in the world. I wanted to work with orphans rescued from sex slavery in Cambodia, and I wanted to write plays protesting the unfair labor practices of Walmart. I volunteered at the exhibit when the AIDS Memorial Quilt was on display. I ran for student government and helped draft a resolution opposing the Iraq War, made anti-war mix CDs for the rallies we held, and attended die-ins.

This is the young woman I was when, in the first semester of my second year, Professor Bob screened PETA's *Meet Your Meat* film for a class on the rhetoric of persuasive arguments. I sat in a college classroom while images I'd never seen, images I hadn't had the capacity to imagine, flickered, slightly grainy and over-pixelated, on the wall in front of me.

Giant metal chutes spat a flurry of white into a caged truck, like laundry, like garbage dumped from the window of an upper-level apartment. The sounds were deafening, a thousand birds tweeting, layered on top and on top of each other, the random bangs of a swinging metal door, the flutter of a thousand pairs of wings.

A suspended black rubber belt orbited a silver tank slowly, white masses dangling, swinging gently. At first, the rotating conveyor belt looked like it was at any other factory. An assembly line.

But then, I realized they were bodies. The white hanging masses. They were chickens, stunned into unconsciousness; they were my frozen, prepackaged, breaded chicken nuggets. And the swinging metal arm that gently brushed up against each body as it passed, so slowly, was actually slitting their throats.

A dancing circle of swinging, dead chickens, wings splayed, spun under its own weight, with gravity, like ten feather dusters gathered at the handle. Over a two-ton vat of purple blood, they hung, swaying in a postmortem ballet.

I watched the images, fading in and out, seeing only flashes: A disembodied hand, from the wrist up, gripped a struggling hen and lifted her to a blue metal gate, a miniature guillotine. A little trap door wrapped itself around the hen's beak, a small movement, like a long slow pinch. It didn't look painful. It didn't look like anything. But the hen tensed, beady black eyes pinched shut, wings flapping frantically, useless yellow-clawed feet scratching at the empty air. When the hen emerged, her once-white beak was pink and bent, half the size and curved downward, drooping towards her chin.

A twitching cow, pushed with a forklift.

A piglet's skull bashed against the concrete floor.

When Professor Bob flipped on the lights at the end of the film, he asked us to comment on the rhetorical strategies at play in the video. I blinked in the harsh light, chewed my lower lip, listened silently.

Professor Bob, my professor and a new mentor, was a vegan, skinny and funny, with a long gaunt face. His typical teaching outfit was khakis and a plaid button-down shirt, and he was perpetually a day behind on shaving, like a slightly polished lumberjack. He'd spent a year digging trenches with the Peace Corps in Kazakhstan, before quitting to return home and marry his wife. They were both volunteers at the local animal shelter, and in addition to full-time teaching jobs, they taught creative writing workshops at a nearby penitentiary. He was a nerd and a smart one, making *Star Wars* reference alongside Jonathan Swift's *A Modest Proposal*, and I thought he and his wife were exactly the kind of adults I hoped to become in college: worldly and opinionated, rife with stories, and able to hold up their end of a political debate at a cocktail party.

In his classroom, I saw something for the first time, and so did many of my classmates. When I tuned back in to the conversation, they were scrambling to come to terms with the violence of the film, to justify their diets, their family farms, their love of bacon.

It's not like that everywhere.

and

My family raises dairy cows.

and

Can they even feel pain?

and

Whatever, steak is good.

and

Protein is good for you.

and

So we should just set the animals free?

and

What about hunting?

and

What about medical testing? That's necessary.

and

What, so we should just all become vegetarian?

Since starting college, I'd been working hard to expand my perspectives: I had recently declared a minor in sociology, and I took classes like Sex and Gender in the Third World, seminars on media and politics. I was a member of the Young Democratic Socialists, the environmental club, the feminist organization, born shiny and new into radical idealism.

But I was starting to come to the uncomfortable realization that I'd never spent any significant amount of time thinking about the fact that food grew somewhere. Food, as far as I was concerned, came from the grocery store. I was used to fluorescent-lit aisles and shrink-wrapped meat, miles of shelves stocked with dozens of brands of chips, and cheese sliced off a massive block by a woman wearing a hairnet.

I thought back to a week in February, when I was seven or eight, that my family spent on a farm in Vermont, the childhood home of my mother's best friend, which was still in operation and run by her parents, Red and Judy. Every morning there, I rose early, peeling back the handmade quilt on the twin-sized bed in the attic, slipping my tiny cold feet into heavy brown boots, and clomping down the stairs, shivering and grinning, to help with chores.

Although at my own house we had a big backyard, thick with rows of spindly pine trees, I was a suburban girl. Our block had fenced-in pools and power lines and a school bus stop in my front yard and a sign that read *Slow Children* (no comma). We played outside often, building tree forts and raking pine needles into houses, and I may have worn red flannel buttondowns, but I was not a farm girl. My week on the farm was a vacation from suburbia, at a magical place where a little girl could carry metal buckets heavy with sap through the snow into the warm sugaring shack to make maple syrup, where she could throw bread to geese that roamed the front yard, where she could pat the warm haunch of a cow on her way to the river.

One morning that week, Judy asked me to help her gather eggs for breakfast. We crunched outside over shorn, frosted grass into a hay-stuffed laying barn, the early-morning geese caws outside muffled by the padded plywood walls. The barn felt warm, insulated, as if I could fall down anywhere and not get hurt, just bounce softly, and giggle. The hens slept hunkered down in laying boxes, feathers puffed, invisible beaks tucked beneath one wing. I watched them inhale and exhale, quivering with slight snores. Judy called them her "little mamas."

"Mama," I whispered into the morning air, the gray smoke of the word drifting slowly away from me in the cold.

Judy handed me a woven wooden basket with a metal handle. "Go ahead," she said.

When I imagine myself in that moment, I laugh a little at the pathetic look on my suburban face, small blonde eyebrows gathered in confusion, static-charged bangs floating over my thick glasses. I had no idea how to gather eggs. Judy showed me, smiling, using the back of her left hand to lift the sleeping hen and her right to reach beneath the body, pulling out a warm, brown-flecked egg. I trembled when I reached beneath my first hen, terrified of the horror I was sure would befall me if I woke the mama hen. But then I held a perfect, smooth egg in my hand and felt the impossible heat emanating from within. We went row by row, filling two buckets with the eggs from just one wall of the laying barn. When I crossed to the other side, Judy shook her head and whispered a gentle no.

"No," she said, "those mamas are hatching."

I only spent a handful of days at the farm as a kid. I barely knew Judy before that day, and I haven't seen her in decades. But when I conjure this memory, I feel an immense gratitude towards her, a childlike sense of protected warmth. Because she let me in on a secret. In that private moment we shared in the laying barn, she pulled back the curtain and took my hand and showed me how something sacred happened.

Red and Judy's farm, it took me fifteen more years to learn, was not what a farm really looks like anymore. Our food was as suburban as my neighborhood, and the result was that I was twenty years old and in college before I saw the kind of farm that raised the meat I ate five nights a week.

IN PROFESSOR BOB'S classroom, one of my classmates raised his hand to speak. He, a skinny vegetarian, was the editor for *Buzzsaw Haircut*, the independent campus magazine for which I occasionally wrote angry op-eds about electoral politics and the media's culture of violence, so when he spoke, I listened. And he said that he really respected people who had the courage to hunt and kill their own meat. That the real problem was how the rest of us got our meat, and how we were reacting to the video.

"I think," he said, "if you turn away from the thought of the death in order to eat meat, you're just letting someone else do the dirty work for you."

And I started to remember things.

I remembered how I hated working at a seafood restaurant in high school, hated the screaming sounds the lobsters made when thrown alive into the pots of boiling water, which all the bearded cooks in the dirty kitchen told me was not, in fact, a scream of pain, but still, I remembered how it scratched its way down my spine and under my skin like fingernails bent backwards.

And I remembered that on my first and only fishing trip, I refused to use bait because I didn't want to kill the worm by stabbing it onto the metal hook, so I caught only a floating piece of cardboard. I remembered the bloody gash through the gill of the fish my friend caught, from where he yanked the hook from its mouth.

But mostly what I thought of, when I sat in Professor Bob's classroom, mulling over the reality of factory farming I had just witnessed, was something my father said once, on a family vacation to London. The five of us sat around a white-clothed table, under silver, dim candlelight flickering in the dark wood-paneled steakhouse in Battersea Park. I pointed, shaking my head, up at the mounted head of a steer on a wooden plaque like a hunting trophy near the room's crown molding.

"Why," I asked my father, "would anyone want to think about the cow while they're trying to enjoy a nice filet mignon?"

"Well," my father replied, "that's what it is."

THAT'S WHAT IT IS, I thought, when I choked on the gruesome images from the PETA movie. When I tried to reconcile my celebratory birthday chicken potpies with the heavy grinding sound of a wood chipper slowed by fifteen thousand squirming bodies tossed in for disposal as mulch, the bodies of chickens too sick for slaughter, too sick to ever be eaten.

The tough rubber of those words in my mind, like ripping the meat off a chicken wing with my teeth, like chewing through it.

It would be another seven years before I ate meat again.

When I was twenty, I watched a video and decided to become a vegetarian. I couldn't stomach what I'd seen. I couldn't be a part of it. Looking back, I see it as an impulse born of youth and indignation, a snap judgment, but I was starting to understand the word "privilege." I was discovering an enormous amount of suffering that happened behind closed doors, in the name of my convenience—cheap clothes and massive landfills and supermarket steaks. This, I realized, was what's been missing from my family's communal approach to food—an acknowledgment of how our choices had an impact beyond our home. And I didn't know what else to do but say no.

I called my mother and told her Thanksgiving had better be good, because it would be my last meal eating meat.

She said, "I am going to have to learn to cook all over again."

JUST A FEW months later, I was drinking cheap beer from cans with Meghan and Caity outside a house beaten by age and heavy partying. We'd met the four men who lived there just a month or so before, at a bar where their band was playing, when we went back to their place and stayed up all night, smoking cigarettes and playing Trivial Pursuit. Now, it was late March, in the middle of a warm streak. The night smelled like the air would burst into bloom. We were punchy in the way people who live through long dark winters get at the first hints of warmth. Aran, the smallest of the boys, short and absolutely covered in tattoos, had just stolen a motorized shopping cart from the grocery store down the street and ridden it the entire two miles back to his house, at about half a mile an hour. He had a lit time bomb inked onto his forearm, the red-orange flame looking as if it burned his skin. He sat in the open windowsill, feet dangling into the night, and watched us.

Meghan was supposed to be giving me a trim with the clippers we'd borrowed from the boys. Like many twenty-year-olds who are angry at the world and don't know where to put it, I had developed an intense love of punk, hardcore, and metal music, and their fuck-you stylings. I'd always kept my hair long, but by the end of my freshman year, my roommate had chopped it off for me—with the scissors from her desk—into a short pixie. Now, this DIY do was getting too long in the back. Some eighties basement-club punk rock was blaring through the open window, and I was sitting on a concrete step with a towel draped around my shoulders when Meghan said, "Hey, do you mind if I try something?"

I bit my lip and looked back over my shoulder at her. "Go for it."

Aran jumped up and scrambled into the house through the window. "Hang on," he shouted over the music and into the night, into our looming summer. "Let me get a before picture!"

The hum of the clippers against my scalp felt good, and I leaned into it, and a few minutes later, all that remained was a thin layer of peach fuzz and bangs. Alone in the dirty bathroom, I leaned towards the skim of the mirror and examined myself: mostly-shaved head, two lip piercings, vegetarian—me. I didn't know yet how I would become the agent of change I so desperately wanted to be, but now I looked the part.

THE NEXT FEW years were a blur of dingy apartments and dingy dorm rooms, gray carpet and any number of obscurely acquired sagging and spotted couches, listening to boys strum acoustic guitars, watching tattooed crowds thrash to loud bands I'd never heard of but moved me to an anger I'd somehow always felt, beginning to think the word "revolution" on a regular basis, new piercings and sociology class discussions, and binges on Smirnoff Ice.

It was in a dorm room the fall after I shaved my head, on a night with warm cheap beer and indie folk music coming from the speakers, showing off my first tattoo—an ampersand between my breasts, to keep it a secret from my parents—that I met the guy who would one day leave me for the West.

He was tall and thin, with glasses with thick brown rims and shaggy ski-bum hair. I'd seen him for months around campus: pilled elbow-patch sweaters from the Salvation Army and a vintage Minolta always around his neck. He seemed to be the perfect blend of sexy and artsy and nerdy when I first laid eyes on him, sitting alone in the dining hall, wearing the hoodie of one of my favorite obscure indie bands, long fingers wrapped around a book. I had a distant lusty crush on him for months before I discovered he—Kevin—shared a dorm room with my friend Matt. The first night we met, as we talked shyly into our cans of Milwaukee's Best, my hopes of starting something up with him flared and then faded, as he told me he planned to leave Ithaca soon, to transfer by the end of the semester to a college in Montana.

Montana might as well have been Mongolia to me. I had never been to Montana, had practically never heard of Montana, so distant and strange its frontier name seemed compared with the quietly padded forests of my northeastern home.

"What's in Montana?" I asked him, thinking his explanation would be practical—he had friends or family there, they offered a major in a program he really wanted to study.

Instead, his face lit up with a smile wide enough to shrug his glasses up on his cheeks, eyes grown distant with fantasy. "Really big mountains," he replied.

I was in love.

And soon, Kevin and I decided we were young enough for a three-month, no-strings-attached, leaving-on-a-jet-plane fling. He had stopped eating red meat years earlier, and within the first month of our dating, he too was a vegetarian. We were all becoming vegetarians then, in our early twenties, in Ithaca and beyond. My high school friends off on their own campuses in New Hampshire and Connecticut and Maine were stumbling across PETA brochures and discovering Thai food and abandoning Tater Tot casserole. We did it just to see if we could, just to see what else would change in our worlds when we discarded our parents' paradigms about what food is, why we ate it, and how it made us feel.

On one winter break at home, Caity told her mother she was considering becoming vegetarian too. Her mother, a short-haired doctor specializing in HIV/AIDS research, who had raised her three daughters in a house where nudity was common, surrounded by an alliance of gay and lesbian artists and poets, sent Caity back to school with her copy of Frances Moore Lappé's *Diet for a Small Planet*. We flipped hungrily through the book, its dog-eared pages unfolding a story we were shocked and appalled to learn. No one had ever told us how wasteful the industrial meat system was, how much land was eaten up by corn and soy to feed cattle whose digestive systems were never meant to eat anything but grass, or how much more tofu could be produced on the same amount of land. In a world we were just beginning to see was so increasingly fueled by greed, in a world of oil and revenge and excess, we couldn't imagine being part of a system that allowed so much hunger. I remember us so clearly, cross-legged on her dorm room bed, reading passages back and forth to each other, while the last season of *Friends* played on the television behind us. I'm not sure we realized the book was written in 1971.

I BEGAN MY foray into vegetarianism in the Ithaca College dining halls, a shining palace where dietary preferences were welcomed and celebrated. Silver chafing dishes warmed kosher entrées, and little laminated cards labeled vegetarian options; the salad bar always had marinated tofu along with tuna and chicken salads. What I didn't know at the time was that the dining halls on my campus were operated by Sodexo, the food services industry giant notorious for its low minimum wage and private prison contracts with the U.S. military.[1] All I saw was the vegan cooking station—its own booth with a separate cooking surface and a chef whose hands were not contaminated with the meat of other dishes.

The vegan station served veggie burgers made with brown rice and black beans. I imagined them soft in someone's hands, rolled around and flattened, the way Nona's raw meatballs felt in my palm before they were baked. A twentysomething Ithaca native with flowers tattooed on the backs of his plastic-gloved hands tossed burgers onto a slatted grill, then wrapped them in red-and-white checked paper and placed them in a cardboard container, next to a side of the coveted sweet potato fries. We loved the Sodexo sweet potato fries, the perfect layer of corn-syrup crispy on the outside, a delicate crust that broke open into the soft, tanning-salon orange flesh of the fry, always just this side of too hot, crumbling and sweet.

Looking back, I suppose I felt I had already done the difficult part: I had made the decision. By giving up meat, I had declared my membership in this new group of budding revolutionaries. We sat around the generic beige tables in our private-school dining hall, us white, upper-middle-class kids with our shaved heads, and discussed serious things, discussed free trade and facial piercings, our naïve fingers shoving handfuls of greasy sweet potato fries into our mouths. We were safe in our convictions. We were happy to let someone else do the cooking.

I HAVE A photograph of myself from around this time, unwashed hair in pigtails glinting red under a late-October sun. I am squinting into the camera, the Washington Monument in the background. Two fingers of my left hand form a V, and in my right hand I hold a poster mounted on a wooden stick, the grayed image of a young girl's body, half-buried in stony rubble, stark white block letters reading, *No Blood for Oil*. And I am smiling.

This was the fall of 2002, my sophomore year, about a month after I stopped eating meat, and my friends and I had driven eight hours through the night from Ithaca to attend a protest in Washington, D.C. When I see the shiny-faced radical optimist in the photograph, I can't help but smile along with her. I feel a surge of pride for the unabashed hope in her expression; I remember the churning in her stomach, the sense of purpose. But I can't look at the beaming smile on her face without also remembering that six months later, despite our protests, President Bush authorized the invasion of Iraq, a war we are still fighting. I became a vegetarian in the swirl of this same controversy, born of the same belief in the power of protest. In the time before the war, decidedly, vocally, against.

But my face in the photograph is not angry, not defiant—it is joyful. I celebrated my boycotts, treasured them as a part of this new, radical identity I was crafting for myself, an identity that I hoped would take me away from the suburban convenience, the enclave of desensitization. The girl in the photograph, who smiled out for peace even as she held the image of a dead body in her hand, looked in only one direction. Outward, forward, away.

IN PREPARATION FOR Christmas dinner later that year, my father and I performed our usual non-cooking-related kitchen duties: inserting the double leaf into the cherrywood table, carefully draping the red-and-green plaid tablecloth over it, laying the real silver flatware alongside the goose-patterned china. We folded the napkins and lined a basket with paper towels for the rolls. Everyone clattered into the kitchen as the last of the food made its way from counter to table. My grandfather, right elbow hiked up over his shoulder, finished carving the roast beef and laid the slices delicately on a large crystal platter. Nana's small knotted fingers gingerly plucked warm Pillsbury crescent rolls from baking sheet to basket. My mother surveyed the scene: she grabbed a spoon for the gravy boat, ladled green beans into the flowered vegetable dish, pointed at my sisters to pour water, wine. Then we sat, the seven of us, around the table in our traditional Christmas seating arrangement, held hands, and bowed our heads to give thanks. All of this, just the same as every year.

But as we began passing full serving platters around the table, or serving each other heaps of mashed potatoes or dripping roast beef, tossing rolls to our neighbors, licking drops of gravy from our fingertips, differences emerged. Dad preferred the ends of the roast, blackened to a crisp on the outside; gray, tough meat on the inside. Caitlin made a little divot in her mashed potatoes and then filled it, a small gravy volcano spilling over the edges. Nana took just two mouthfuls of everything, nothing more, and wouldn't finish even that. Gampi loved the fat and gristle of the roast, keeping it in the corner of his mouth and gnawing long after the meal was done. And my plate that year held two crescent rolls, several forkfuls of green beans, and an extra-large serving of mashed potatoes. No meat, no gravy, not this time.

This was my first Christmas as a vegetarian, the first ceremonial family meal since I'd stopped eating meat, and I was not at all prepared for the alienation I felt sitting at that table, looking around at the others' plates, passing meat along, smiling awkwardly at my own sisters as if apologetic. I finished eating before everyone else for the first time in my life and saw then how unlike the rest of my family I had become.

My whole life, my family had believed that the dinner table was a place you came together, that eating was a crucial, collective activity. But when I sat, pierced and protesting, at my family's Christmas dinner table that year, I remembered the little girl building a fort of books to shield herself from the kitchen noise, the nights with pizza and my father. When I imagined myself through their eyes, a newborn radical fresh home from her hippie college, bearing strange new habits and restrictions, I didn't think they understood anything I did anymore. And I took that as a challenge. Tension in my shoulders, I settled into the role of outsider. Perhaps, I thought, this was inevitable, that the redheaded eldest daughter would one day splinter apart from her Italian family heritage.

Food had been the bedrock of my family, the solid foundation onto which all of our connection was built, the means of expression, the reason. When I discovered the bloody, complex truth behind our family meals, the battery cages and the electric stunners. I saw cracks in what I thought had been a solid foundation. I decided to build my own.

Chapter Four

Cheez Whiz Is Vegetarian

I **WAS SITTING AT** the kitchen table with my new roommate, Erin, in Washington, D.C. She had a map of the city and a red Sharpie she was using to circle neighborhoods I should avoid. I was new to the city, a recent and hopeful college graduate, staying with some friends of a friend from high school for the duration of my summer internship with an environmental nonprofit. Erin had spent the last four years studying at George Washington University and wanted to make sure I could navigate the dense, complex city comfortably on my own. Here, she circled, was a great coffee shop on my way back from work. She marked Ben's Chili Bowl and Kramerbooks and an independent record store where she knew I'd be able to find the kinds of obscure bands we both liked. Meridian Hill Park, just blocks from our apartment, was fine and beautiful during the day, but there had been a recent string of sexual assaults there after dark. Columbia Heights, the next neighborhood to the west, was a known drug hub. Needles in the street.

This was my introduction to the city, a place full of art and politics, of potential and promise—for the right people, in the right place, at the right time.

SHORTLY BEFORE MY college graduation, determined not to move back in with my parents, I'd gotten an internship with the Communications Department at the Wilderness Society, practically a dream job for a young activist writer. I arrived at the office on my first day—one week and two days after my college graduation ceremony—with feet blistered from the heels I'd walked in for three blocks from the bus stop. The building, the whole block, stretched before me like an urban dream, my Mary Tyler Moore fantasy come to life. Smooth taupe bricks, an enormous window etched with the Wilderness Society's logo in gold, a courtyard dotted with blossoming cherry trees, and a stone archway marking the entrance. Directly across the street, I could see the fountain and sunken amphitheater courtyard of the National Geographic Society. I took a deep breath, ignoring the faint sweet rot of a mid-Atlantic city in the summer, and thought, *This is it.* I was living confidently in the direction of my dreams. My real life could begin.

My nervousness at meeting the people I'd only spoken to over the phone was unfounded. Within the first few weeks, I'd become comfortable and familiar with my coworkers: Pete, one of the three vice-presidents for communications, a kind father to a toddler daughter, with a beard and glasses, a man who looked like he spent his weekends in wool socks and hiking boots; Drew, a funny and sensible law school grad, just a few years older than me, who would leave in the fall to join his fiancée on a yearlong Fulbright to Lima; and later, Sharon, a young Korean American in the year between American

University and Georgetown Law, with whom I gossiped regularly in the office.

My first task, after getting settled in, was to write a series of press releases, based on a template, about some of the monuments in the National Landscape Conservation System, a lesser-known, less-protected series of parks run by the Bureau of Land Management. The language of advocacy was already in the press releases, the result of months of focus groups and messaging meetings. My job was to write a brief paragraph about the beauty and conservation value of each monument so that we could personalize the press release by state: the Canyons of the Ancients in Colorado, Grand Staircase-Escalante in Utah, Upper Missouri River Breaks in Montana. I spent my first few weeks as a college graduate studying photographs and fact sheets about some of the most beautiful wild places in the country and describing what I saw. This was perfect.

ONE NIGHT THAT summer, I returned home to my apartment around ten at night and realized I hadn't eaten anything all day. Dizzy and grouchy and tired, I yanked open the door to my freezer and cupboards, tossing a series of cardboard boxes onto the counter. I ripped open the tab on a package of Near East Parmesan-flavored couscous and poured the grain into a plastic bowl. I sliced open the seasoning packet and dumped the white powder flecked with dried green herbs into the water, stirring quickly with a fork before setting the whole thing in the microwave to rotate on its glass plate. A fake chicken patty slipped from its cellophane sleeve straight into the toaster for a minute on each side. Ten minutes later, I sat cross-legged on our hand-me-down orange couch, a plastic dinner plate balanced on my lap, watching Martin Sheen play the president on TV and swirling fake meat through a small pond of ranch dressing.

This is what passed for a meal most of my first few years as a vegetarian. I was still young, capable of eating anything short of Tupperware and remaining healthy. I had no clue about budgeting for groceries. And I had spent most of my childhood hiding beneath a table, avoiding the feminine domestic, which is to say: I never really learned how to cook. Cracks began to form in my perfect activist adulthood.

The problem with being a vegetarian, I discovered, was that you couldn't eat meat. Steak was my favorite food when I was seventeen—I couldn't get enough of that tough, chewy meat, of the red-gray flesh peeling apart into moist strands under the pressure and slide of a knife. I'd let each bite drip bloody juice onto my mashed potatoes before I ate it, sucking the meat dry in the corner of my mouth. But being a vegetarian meant you had to eat a lot of vegetables, and I'd never really been a fan.

I gagged over the grimy paste of lentils mashed between the flat plates of my teeth, the slimy flesh of an eggplant slipping towards the back of my throat, the grainy pulp of a soft pear. Broccoli tasted like plastic to me, hummus like dirt. I couldn't so much as graze the fuzzed skin of a peach against my lower lip without convulsing in a shiver of disgust. Once, in a nice restaurant in California, I accidentally put a slice of mushroom into my mouth—masked under the thick Alfredo sauce on my manicotti, which I had ordered *without* mushrooms—and the gritty edges of it, the slickness against my tongue, made me so sick I had to run to the bathroom to spit it out into a trash can.

When I decided to become a vegetarian, I abandoned my family's communal learning space. Stepping outside of my family kitchen meant I'd left behind any chance to learn what to do when faced with a diet dictated by unknown ingredients. Like most twentysomethings left to fend for themselves, I learned to cook cheap and easy. I just did it without meat. I ate basically the same diet as I had as a non-vegetarian, subtracting the meat and filling in the white space left on my plate with more of the something else. Think frozen pizzas. Think Tater Tots and cheese sandwiches. Think instant ramen. Lots and lots of instant ramen (only the mysteriously named "Oriental" flavor, without beef or chicken fat). Kraft's blue boxes of dried macaroni and powdered cheese are vegetarian friendly and only about sixty cents apiece. After a few years, I became adventurous enough to branch into the "ethnic" food aisles at the grocery store, tossing cans of refried beans, flour tortillas, salsa, and pre-shredded cheese into the cart for quesadillas. Boxed rice, boxed couscous, boxes risotto mixes.

I never really added produce.

When I discovered meat substitute products, they were a godsend. No longer did I have to pretend a meal without meat was filling. Now I had fake steak strips for fajitas, fake chicken patties to eat between hamburger buns with ranch dressing, fake chicken breasts to toss into a stir-fry, Tofurky and soy and mycoprotein molded into new shapes.

A few years later, I saw an episode of *The Biggest Loser*, NBC's weight loss show, during which their personal trainer took the contestants grocery shopping with a nutritionist. The muscular trainer stood, midriff bared, alongside the trim blonde nutritionist in her blue polo as she told the group they should do most of their grocery shopping around the perimeter of the store, because that's where the "real" food is located: the deli and butcher for meat and cheese, the bakery for fresh breads, the produce section. Avoid the middle, she told them. This is where the processed food—highest in calories, lowest in nutritional value—lives.

I did my grocery shopping at eight o'clock on Sunday nights in the neighborhood Safeway, beneath a sign alerting me to constant surveillance of this street corner as a known drug exchange. And I did all of my shopping at the center of the store, weaving a sparse cart up and down aisles of boxed food, canned food, frozen food. But at least I wasn't eating meat.

D.C. HAD NEVER been my plan. When I finished college with a writing degree, I hoped to find freelance work in Montana. Kevin and I had stayed together when he moved west, but after a year and a half, the distance was putting a strain on our relationship. Openings for writers were slim anywhere, let alone in a small Western town, and when I found the internship at the Wilderness Society, I was just smart enough to realize I couldn't afford to turn it down for a guy. Despite all this, I fell in instant love with the city, where culture seemed to light a match beneath radical politics, igniting it with color and dancing flames. Impromptu drum circles flared up in the middle of Meridian Hill every early Sunday evening, my neighbors dancing in brightly colored clothes as the last slants of sunlight faded behind dense trees. When Kevin came for occasional weekend visits, we strolled through the Smithsonian's museums, drank white wine with brunch, sat at the edge of the Lincoln Memorial, and watched the sun set into the reflecting pool. I took yoga classes in a basement-level studio painted purple and run by two women whose black labs meditated with us. I stayed out late on the weekends, ears ringing from shrill guitars amplified through massive speakers as independent rock bands played cheap shows at the 9:30 Club or the Black Cat.

My roommates and I were all young idealists, four girls in a two-bedroom apartment with a view of the Washington Monument, swapping stories from our various nonprofit day jobs: providing microloans to farmers in Southeast Asia and escorting pregnant women past the picket lines at Planned Parenthood. One of my responsibilities as a communications intern was the "hill-drop," where I literally walked the halls of Congress, knocking on the doors of senators and representatives to ask if I could drop off a memo about preserving wilderness for future generations. I felt at home and purposeful. In a letter to a friend, I described my job as "the real deal," a marriage of writing and activist passions.

The city was like a bolt of lightning: brief and luminous, electric. One Friday afternoon I had off from work, the skies burst open with a sudden hot rainstorm. Thunder shook the building and wind whipped bare tree branches down the empty gray streets. I opened up our fourth-story living room window and sat on the ledge, closing the window over my face to protect the room from the water and myself from my fear of heights, and let my bare legs dangle out into the summer rain.

A GRAFFITI CAMPAIGN sprung up around the city that summer, a single four-letter word spray-painted all over our Northwest neighborhood, on metro station walls and cement park trash cans and stone pillars around Dupont Circle: *BORF*. For most of the summer, I didn't know what it meant, just saw the word as it grew, lacing itself around the city. In mid-July, a young student at a city art school was arrested on a tip and made to explain himself. "Borf," he said, was the nickname of his friend Bobby Fisher, whose image he had also used in stencil, a friend who had committed suicide by hanging when he was sixteen.

The campaign was an homage, a mourning but, most of all, an act of outrage, the frenzied, messy, artistic expression of a group of students who had nowhere to put all their hurt.

In a video piece released the next year, the Borf Brigade, as they had by then become known, spoke over images of secret stenciling: "This epidemic cannot be medicated into remission. It is not a problem confined to our family bloodline. 'Trouble at home' is not the only trigger for depression."[1] Although seeing the mysterious letters on traffic lights and skate park slopes was always a little thrill, a discovery, once the story came out, the whole campaign seemed haunted, a reminder that there were forces at work in this city that I could only guess at, could barely see.

One night, some friends gathered at the apartment of my roommate's boyfriend and his brother, the two of them sharing a studio in a secure building in Columbia Heights. We played Scrabble, ate cheese with wine, played at being thinking, cultured adults. I wandered around the small, single room they shared, admiring the construction-paper artwork on their walls. Red smears on a yellow sheet of paper. Thick black lines on green. One of the residents of the apartment was an art teacher at an elementary school in Southeast D.C. He explained that these were portraits he'd asked his second-grade students to draw: the red smears were how they painted the view outside their apartment windows; the thick black lines were drawn by one boy when he was asked for a portrait of his father, in prison.

In the summer of 2005, we were two years into a war I had protested on these streets, on the same streets where some of these children lived, on Martin Luther King Jr. Avenue, where rock attacks on buses were so common drivers were advised to wear safety goggles. The Southeast quadrant of D.C., where my friend worked, had a population that was more than 90 percent African American, only two grocery stores per ward, and diabetes rates higher and household incomes lower than anywhere else in the district.[2] Just blocks from the White House, where I had once marched.

The heat of a mid-Atlantic summer oppresses slowly and softly, a heavy wet blanket of lethargy that spreads gradually, first up over your legs and then onto your shoulders. Finally, your chest heaving in sleep, you're unable to breathe through the weight. We didn't have air conditioning, so we slept with the windows flung wide open, the sirens and shouts of 18th Street echoing into our dreams.

In mid-July, the nonprofit I worked for threw a company picnic. We drove a fleet of rented vans to Maryland's Rock Creek Park, about an hour away, and spent the day grilling hot dogs and veggie burgers, playing volleyball, wandering by bike or on foot the loops of wooded trails. Almost as soon as we arrived, a few other employees and I walked down to the edge of a small river running through the park, to a patch of warm sand where we could take off our shoes and wade in. I stood ankle-deep in the cool water, my toes curled and digging into wet, murky sand, and realized this was the first time I'd stood outside, barefoot, all summer long.

Summers growing up had always been barefoot: the burn of hot pavement, the tickling of cool grass, the stickiness of dripping fruit juice popsicles. But now, rather than playing outside, letting my toes burrow into the soil, I was spending my summer, cardigan shrugged over my shoulders against the office air conditioning, phone pressed to my ear, speaking to unknown reporters in Montana on behalf of the great outdoors. Over the last eight weeks, I'd researched and written about some of the most beautiful, exotic wild places in the United States: the archaeological treasures still undiscovered in Colorado's Canyons of the Ancients, the sunset striations on the stones of Utah's Grand Staircase. But I'd been staring at a photo on a computer screen. How would I visit them? When would my palms know the warmth of that rock, if I continued working for them, in the city?

HERE'S HOW IT should have worked: I became a vegetarian. I began trying new vegetables: asparagus and leeks and bean sprouts. I used only cloth grocery bags. I shopped entirely at the local farmers market. I learned to bake my own bread, white knuckles kneading fresh dough daily, or how to make my own cheese, weaving long rubbery braids of mozzarella. Through my food, I communed with the landscape around me, raising my own diet up from the soil, cradling little green pots of basil, chives, cilantro in the warm light of a kitchen window-sill, constructing a raised bed out back and planting rows of sweet red peppers. I walked amid my produce, fingers running lightly along tomatoes staked in the ground, their green vines reaching towards the blue sky like hope. Yellow squash and cucumber flowered along the ground, their spiky skin pricking my hands as I picked them every Saturday morning in the sun.

But that's not how it worked. I ate frozen, microwave-ready meals, vegetarian tofu potpies topping a thousand calories per individual serving. I didn't even think about the bleached flour and sugar in my processed white bread, the chemicals in Miracle Whip, or the sodium content of fake bologna slices. Potato chips and Cheez Whiz were vegetarian, not to mention cheap. I heated and reheated chemical compounds, oblivious to the carcinogenic potential of red dye #40.

I had the best intentions, but I was a child of the suburbs, changing my diet without changing any world view. These meals were ethical by only one standard—no meat—vegetarian by technicality. In college, being a vegetarian seemed easy—I was surrounded by young upper-middle-class suburban radicals, most of them vegetarian. My boyfriend was a vegetarian. The campus dining hall had a vegan station. Here in the city, I was eating bad food because I couldn't cook for myself, and I was alone. I was living the reality of most people in inner-city environments—fresh, healthy produce was difficult to find, and either of poor quality or too expensive to afford when I did. And the fake meat products that became my dietary crutch were chemical creations with a big environmental impact. I began to feel overwhelmed by how much work it was going to take to live and eat true to these ethical ideals. I wasn't well prepared for what vegetarianism or postgraduate life would entail.

ONE NIGHT, I went out into the city alone, to wander along the neon signs of 18th Street, smoking cigarettes—which I smoked for years without realizing how incongruous they were with my goals for a healthy, vegetarian lifestyle—and feeling despondent. Lost. I don't think I admitted it to myself then, but the city was too much for me. Sure, I'd learned plenty about poverty in college, but I couldn't handle seeing it up close, in the stark reality of limited food access and homelessness and addiction. I wandered the streets and thought about leaving, wondered whether leaving would make me a hypocrite.

A man rode a bicycle towards me on the sidewalk, plastic grocery bags slung heavily over both handlebars, the gray hood of his sweatshirt pulled up and masking his face. Although the sidewalk was wide, I stepped aside to let him pass. But as he rode by, frustrated with the awkward dance of who-goes-which-way, he barked, "Bitch, I'm not in your way!"

I barely made it back to my apartment without crying. The man on the bicycle had seen an out-of-her-element white girl, a scared upper-middle-class girl pressed against the side of a building by a black man on the street. I wasn't that girl—or I didn't think I was, or I didn't want to be. I hadn't stepped aside because of the color of his skin. But I knew I lived in a different world now, one burdened by the reality that I needed more than good intentions. Becoming a vegetarian had been a gesture of activism, but putting it into practice was more difficult than I'd expected. Moving to a city was what I thought I wanted, but I felt lonely and out of my depth. When I think about it now, I see my liberal privilege exposed, no longer sheltered by the safe confines of a college classroom, or the sterilized enclave of a suburb.

I couldn't quite put my finger on it, but there was something complicated about the city: something uncomfortable in the space between the progressive I wanted to be and the discomfort I felt walking through Columbia Heights at night. I was living in the midst of systemic poverty and institutional racism, and deep down I knew that no amount of boycotting, no well-organized rally, could fix that. I also felt a little hypocritical. I worked in an upscale air-conditioned office, cold-calling reporters and putting together press events to raise money and awareness for wild spaces that were as far removed from this city as possible. How many children from that Southeast elementary school would ever visit Zion National Park? Did the work I was doing matter, in the context of the crime rates and rampant addiction right outside my door?

When my roommates asked me what was wrong that night, I was too embarrassed to tell them that a man on a bicycle had yelled at me, so instead I just said, "The city makes me sad." Knowing that they, in their liberal hearts, would understand, I told them, "There's so much broken here."

I began to daydream about the West, a place where I could escape these messy complications. A place, I thought, where I could live fully: where there would be easy access to the local food and fresh produce I knew I needed to be a better vegetarian, where it would cost less to live and I would have more time to write, where there was more space to wander and fewer people, where maybe I could dig down deep and truly join the community. I set my sights again on Montana, where Kevin was still in college, where I could start over.

ONE AFTERNOON IN August, I sat on a lawn in front of the Capitol Building with my coworkers Pete and Drew. Sitting in the shade to avoid the midday sun, we ate sandwiches out of Tupperware containers we'd packed from home. We were about to hold a rally to announce the newly formed campaign, backed by a coalition of all the D.C. environmental nonprofits, to fight the Bush administration's push to drill in the Arctic National Wildlife Refuge. A man in a polar bear costume waited in the air conditioning inside, so as to avoid suffering heatstroke before he had to make his press photo–worthy appearance. As we chatted, Pete told me they'd loved having me and offered to extend my internship into the fall. I smiled and told him thanks but no thanks. I'd loved working there, too, but had made up my mind that Montana would fit me better, would be a place I could live the wild and unconventional life I wanted.

I told myself I had to decide which side of the door I wanted to be on. I could stay in D.C., and I knew I could succeed. I could work my way up the environmental nonprofit ladder, lobbying Congress and assuming a wardrobe of kitten heels and pantsuits, planning rallies and cold-calling reporters for coverage, maybe even someday scheduling my own press conference. I thought of this as working for change from within the system—playing the political game.

Or, I decided, I could step away. I could stay on the outside. I wanted to live as an artist, a life of joyful solitude out in the mountains, writing the beauty of the wilderness across pages that would inspire others to act on its behalf, banging on the door for change from the outside, as loud and raucous and uncompromising as I wanted. The city had dirtied my ideal, complicated it, but I wasn't ready to give up hope. I chose, again, to leave, to turn away. I headed west.

IN LATE AUGUST, just before I left the city, a friend from college called to say she would be in town to interview for her own future internship and asked if I wanted to grab dinner and catch up. When Kate arrived at my apartment, she was so excited to have passed a restaurant called Meskerem on her way up the block, saying she'd always wanted to try Ethiopian food. As the dutiful hostess, I agreed. In sandals and shorts, we perched on leather stools around a small red table and let the waiter order for us, the sting of red pepper in my nostrils.

I had no reason to believe I would like Ethiopian food. Just sitting in the restaurant, I felt like a trespasser, like I'd hitchhiked along on one of my mother's girls' nights out, like I'd never wanted to, certain I would embarrass myself by clattering with strange utensils, gagging, sweating with the spiciness of the food. But I couldn't admit this fear to Kate, couldn't acknowledge that I was still just the white suburban girl afraid to try new things. A picky eater gets used to fighting through visceral reactions to food so as to not disrupt social situations.

Plus, admitting in this small way that I was afraid to try something new would, I feared, give me away; it would mean acknowledging I was leaving the city because I was scared.

My fear intensified as the waiters in loose white shirts and maroon slacks brought our dinner on large metal platters and stayed to explain the dishes. *Gomen wat*, steaming wilted collard greens stewed in berbere, a blend of spices including hot red pepper. *Kik alicha*, a soupy yellow substance: split peas simmered in an onion sauce. *Misir azifa*, a salad of finely chopped onion, green chilies, and pureed lentils. Unfamiliar ingredients and heavy spice. My stomach turned nervously.

For many of my childhood friends, leaving New Hampshire and going out into the wide world was their first opportunity for exposure, the first chance they had to meet people from other regions and try other foods. A city friend takes you out for sushi. A Texan friend cooks black-eyed peas, tamales. An Iranian roommate brings home a pomegranate. Somehow, they were born with a willingness to the world, the ability to open themselves to new ideas and experiences. They were unafraid, unabashed, welcoming. They did not hide their newness. They celebrated it.

My mother gave me these opportunities: exotic, cultural, international. I knew what chicken tikka masala was before I was twelve, had tried her summer tabbouleh salad in a pita, her homemade tahini sauce. But before I ever left my parents' house, my walls were up. Where my friends saw possibility, an abundance of ingredients, a source of experimentation and growth, I shrank in fear, my taste buds too sensitive, too stubborn. I wasn't interested in trying new things if they would just make me gag. New languages, new foods didn't excite me—they made me nervous. I never allowed myself to imagine I could belong.

But the waiters began to lead us in a demonstration of Ethiopian eating technique, and the anthropologist in me turned on, leaned in slightly to get a better look, curious about cultural phenomena. They broke off pieces of the injera, a kind of floppy crepe, a spongy flatbread, and used it as a utensil to scoop up bites of each dish straight into their mouths. No silverware. Lots of sharing. Concern over the alien foods gave way to an eager desire to try something new, to the novelty of eating sloppily and loudly, with my hands, in a public place. We followed the waiters' demonstrations, giggling awkwardly, turning to our neighboring tables to laugh together. The waiters encouraged us to interact with other customers, explaining that cross-table sharing was common, extending the notion of family-style entrées. Later, when business slowed, they returned to our table, laughing at our messiness, wrapping their hands around ours, helping to guide the spicy foods into our inexperienced mouths.

D.C. has the highest concentration of Ethiopians anywhere in the United States—more than 150,000 immigrants in a ten-square-mile city.[3] In fact, the city boasts the largest Ethiopian population anywhere in the world outside of Ethiopia itself. That night at Meskerem, I sensed this abundance, felt it wrap around me, the ease with which an uncomfortable outsider was welcomed in.

The menu at Meskerem explains sharing injera as more than just an eating technique. Eating from the same plate, or breaking injera together, symbolizes the bonds of loyalty and friendship. When two people share a plate, they demonstrate their respect for one another, through the connection inherent in trusting each other with food. The act connects person to person, as well as person to food, removing the sterile boundary of the fork, or of separate plates. The height of this connection is *gursha*—the act of placing food from one's own hand into another's mouth.

I understood in my blood the tenderness of feeding the ones you love. My great-grandmother's hands sank deep into the food that went straight into our mouths. No sterility. No gloves while rolling meatballs, while carrying spaghetti. Her food was a consecration, a gift for someone else. When I watched other people in the restaurant that night, I wasn't thinking of the ritual of giving food to another, because this I understood. What fascinated me was the opening of the self, the trust of welcoming another's hand into your mouth, the willingness to come into contact with the whole world, safe or not.

Chapter Five

Elk Country, Part I

ONE WARM OCTOBER afternoon just a few months later, I was piercing price tags through the furry skins of stuffed bison and T-shirts with clever sayings about moose, chatting with my new coworker Maggie. Maggie was a small sixteen-year-old native Montanan with long mousy brown hair always in a ponytail, talkative and eager in her green polo shirt, working Saturdays to pad her savings account before college. We took to each other quickly and spent hours talking about books. On this day, she was telling me that her dream was to return to Montana after college and get a little piece of land in Belgrade, with its dense hunting cover and memories of home. Lost in a reverie, she asked me if I'd ever tried venison.

"No," I replied, casually, unguarded. "I'm a vegetarian."

And Maggie said, "What? Oh. I... I don't think I can be friends with a vegetarian."

I'd only been in Bozeman, a lively college town in the southwest corner of Montana, for about a month, but because I only had three months before I had to start making payments on my undergraduate student loans, I took the first job I could get, unpacking boxes and pricing items in the basement of a souvenir shop downtown. And because the gift shop I worked in was targeted towards tourists, I'd become accustomed to being taken as an expert on the daily workings of the town in which I was myself a recent transplant. I knew where to find the best burger in town (the Garage) and whether the Museum of the Rockies was open on Saturdays (yes, ten to four). I could give directions to the nearest post office (three blocks south, one west). I could fake a response about the "sick pow" at Bridger (as I was not then, nor have I yet become, a skier). I may have just moved to Bozeman, but I didn't think of myself as an interloper. I planned to stay. I was a resident: comfortable, at home.

When I asked Maggie why she couldn't be friends with a vegetarian, her response hinted at the chasm between us, the ways in which our different childhoods in different geographies would dictate our ability to share this community.

"Well," she said, "it's just... I learned to skin and gut an elk when I was thirteen."

This was the moment I began to think of myself as an outsider in the Rockies.

TELLING PEOPLE I was a vegetarian in Bozeman was like strapping on a scarlet letter. In the three years since I'd declared my independence from meat, I'd only had to manage that diet in a liberal, wealthy, college town and an East Coast city. Although my family was confused by my choice, they accommodated it. Until I lived in Montana, it had never occurred to me that anyone would consider this a genuinely weird decision. In my limited world view, where tofu was standard on restaurant menus and access to veggie burgers was abundant, vegetarian-ism was one of many dietary choices. In Montana, people were surprised when I told them I didn't eat meat, as if they'd heard of such a thing but had never actually seen anyone stupid enough to fall for the idea. I can hardly remember eating out at restaurants in Montana—when I do, I recall meals cobbled together from salads and appetizers. Parmesan cheese fries and a game of pool at Montana Ale Works, a cheese sandwich at the Pickle Barrel, plain cheese pizza at MacKenzie River.

One night, a friend gave me a gift certificate to a restaurant in rural Logan called the Land of Magic Dinner Club, a short thirty-minute drive from Bozeman into the Crazies, a north-ern Rocky Mountain range. Kevin and I were enamored of the restaurant's name and talked excitedly on the drive there, imagining little gnomes and other strange creatures as our waiters. The parking lot of the Land of Magic Dinner Club was unpaved, and the tires of Kevin's Subaru kicked up loose dust as he parked beside a pickup truck. A man was selling pit bull puppies out of the back.

Inside, Kevin and I puzzled over the menu and paused awkwardly before confirming with each other—not a sin-gle vegetarian item was to be found there. When the waitress came to take our order and we explained our predicament, she laughed out loud at the word "vegetarian." We ordered baked potatoes, sides of steamed vegetables, side salads, an expensive bottle of wine, and a whole chocolate cake to go, slinking out, we hoped, without attracting too much attention.

I ACCLIMATED TO Bozeman more slowly than I'd expected. I was unaccustomed to the feeling of wanting to stay in a place, and I didn't yet quite know how to make a home. Working at the souvenir shop helped me get my feet wet in the West, and in becoming a new resident in a new town. I'd spent a few months visiting Kevin in Bozeman the previous summer and had started freelancing for a local outdoor magazine. I found a strange apartment: the furnished bottom half of a split-level ranch house, whose owner had installed a door at the base of the stairs that separated us, and where I watered my landlord's plants upstairs when he went to Thailand for a month that fall. When I moved in, I had almost nothing: no kitchen supplies, no vacuum cleaner, no lamps or chairs or pillows—only two suitcases full of books and clothes.

I spent the first few months in a temporary job, without a car, walking the mile to work each morning around sunrise. Eventually, I inched my way towards something more permanent and stable: working as a development assistant for the local animal shelter. I organized fundraisers and wrote grants and an endless string of thank-you notes to every person who sent us a check in the mail.

Since Kevin was still a college student—his nights full of organic chemistry lab reports and studying for agronomy exams—dinner became our one guaranteed nightly ritual, the time we could always spend together. We had very little money, little time, and barely any cooking ability, but I did my best to craft the appearance of an elaborate dinner from limited resources: cheap, easy vegetarian food with paper towel napkins, little bowls of ranch dressing beside our frozen pizza and Tater Tots, fresh Parmesan cheese grated on top of boxed macaroni. I played at a domestic life even while I was a visitor in his house, dancing around his roommates as they dumped whole cans of chili into plastic microwaveable bowls and ate standing up in the kitchen. I longed to feed him: for the purpose, the connection.

But I worried it could become a slippery slope from cooking out of love to cooking out of obligation. I wondered, in a distant corner of my mind, whether I was becoming a housewife, whether I was giving too much of myself to him. If feeding others made me so content, would it end up tying me down? Would it stop me from leaving if I wanted to, give me the sense of abandoning someone who needed me? Could I feed myself, too?

When I did eat alone, at my own apartment, usually I boiled packets of ramen in a single-serving saucepan and ate at the kitchen table, a book propped in front of me for company.

AS AUTUMN DESCENDED across Montana, I felt the first pangs of nostalgia, an unfamiliar homesickness for which I was unprepared, having always been eager to leave home. Autumn in the Northeast, my autumn, was a flare gun, all brilliant flaming leaves and pumpkin-carving contests and days up in the green branches of the U-pick apple orchard—a distant memory now. Harvest rituals embedded even into my suburban childhood made fall the time I felt most closely tied to the land, the thick pine forests and rocky soil of New England.

The only trees that changed color in Bozeman were the cottonwoods, and so the mountains remained draped in green into October. Most of the people of my new home connected to their land in two primary ways: skiing and hunting. Autumn, which had been to me a ritual unto itself, became the time of praying for the first big snow and the thrill of open season.

Suddenly, everyone around me knew how to gut a fish, fire a gun, take a life. Neighbors hung deer by their hooves in small suburban garages. Stiff legs poked out of the backs of pickup trucks at gas stations. The head of a bobcat hung on the wall of my favorite bar. I toured Yellowstone National Park in October to watch the majesty of the elk rut, to hear the lows and snorts of great animals and smell the steam rising off their sweating bodies. The entrance attendant warned me to wear bright colors and stay near the roads. Montanans went to kill the elk, when males were easier targets while distracted by the single-minded need to mate.

Hunting, before Montana, had been much like farming, an idea I thought of as something from times past. Although people hunted in New Hampshire, I knew hunters only as the echoes of a boom in the backyard, as the flashes of orange, and as the reason I couldn't play out in the woods in October. The men of my family, what few there are, did not own guns or spend wet Saturdays hunkered down in blinds, waiting for the pass of brown across binoculars. My forest was a safe place, a place of ground-level forts and Peter Pan fantasies, of sword fights on fallen logs across small brooks, more pine needle than pines, hiding nothing wilder than the occasional garter snake. The only blood on my parents' hands dripped there while they were repackaging frozen steaks bought in bulk from Costco into multiple ziplock bags. We may have had a forested backyard, but we didn't live in the woods—we lived right up against the edge.

The hunt, to the Montanans I knew that first autumn, represented tradition. For Maggie, and many others, this was a lifelong memory, a tradition that went back generations, a lesson a child was meant to learn. In the woods with a gun, the children of Montana learned to acknowledge just how close this place still was to being, at any moment, overrun by the wild. The skills to take down an animal and dismantle a kill memorialized the long struggle to settle the frontier, the hard times so recently passed when these animals offered themselves to the building of this part of the country. Hunting was part of a history lesson, and a romanticized one, the history of conquest and Manifest Destiny, of European settlers "taming the wild frontier."

That fall, I thought back to my distant New York college classroom, and to my vegetarian classmate, speaking of his respect for hunters. I had somehow thought of hunting then as kind of noble, as a way of communing with nature, and I had opted out of meat eating because I couldn't bear to look at it. I tried to imagine myself slitting an animal's throat and turned away in disgust. In Montana, I saw what I had been afraid of. The blood-and-guts reality of a dead animal was a foreign language I couldn't translate. To me, the gun seemed less a way of communing with nature than a celebration of having conquered her, the trophy of nature's defeat. When I saw the bare flesh, when I smelled its disintegration, when I saw what it really looked like when an animal died, I found I didn't have the stomach for all that death.

IN NOVEMBER OF that year, a teenager in the next town over shot and killed the first legally hunted American bison in the state of Montana in more than fifteen years, on the second day of Montana's newly reinstated bison season. I read the account in the daily paper that flopped onto my front walkway in the early-morning hours. Buddy Clement, one of just fifty people to whom the state had offered hunting tags for bison that year, fired the kill shot into the animal's head from about thirty yards away, in plain sight of the bull, no more than a mile's hike from the nearest paved road. Clement had been led to the kill site by an official with the Montana Department of Fish, Wildlife and Parks, who had issued the permits in the hope of maintaining a target population for the growing restored wild bison heard of southwest Montana.[1]

As an outsider, someone whose family had not participated in frontier history, I couldn't reconcile the logic of hunting bison with the animal's history in the American West. From where I stood, with no gun in hand, I couldn't separate the modern bison hunt from its context of European settlers and Native Americans, the struggle of conquest and colonization. When I sat in Montana, at our dining room table cut to look like a slab of a fallen tree, reading the 250-word piece about Buddy Clement's kill, I remembered the accounts I'd read in history books, pursuing my long-distance crush on the Rocky Mountains with research, with information gathering, with fact.

I remembered that bison were hunted nearly to extinction in the nineteenth century, their numbers dwindling from an estimated 60 million before 1800 to a few hundred.[2] The value of a bison's kill to a European settler came from its hide, a commodity that needed to be obtained in large numbers to turn a profit. A good hide could earn three dollars, and a very good hide topped out around fifty, in an era during which a day laborer was lucky to bring home a dollar. Bands of hunters rode out onto the plains, capable of killing a hundred animals a day. A skin team used sledgehammers to spike the animal's nose to the ground, then hooked up the horse team and pulled the hide off the dead body. Riding off to the next kill, the team would leave the carcass to rot in the sun. After a few weeks, once the sun had dried the muscle to leather, once scavengers had picked clean the skeleton, the outfit would return to harvest the last scraps of the body, collecting the barren bones to ship back east, to become knife handles, glue, decor.

In the latter part of the century, there were nearly a thousand such outfits in operation.

But there was another crucial advantage to the mass slaughter of American bison by European settlers: the eradication of Plains Native American tribes. Since so much of the tribes' livelihood depended upon the bison, which they used for food, clothing, shelter, and much more, U.S. military leaders actively encouraged bison hunting outfits. They knew that as bison became scarcer, it would become easier to round indigenous people up and force them onto reservations, clearing the land for white settlement. General William Tecumseh Sherman once remarked that "the quickest way to compel the Indians to settle down to civilized life was to send ten regiments of soldiers to the plains, with orders to shoot buffaloes until they became too scarce to support the redskins."[3]

This was the legacy I recalled when I read Montana had reopened bison hunting season, a history of conquest, defeat, near-extinction. Buddy Clement's bison didn't even know he was prey. The hunt required no chase. There was, as I saw it, no great ritual of predator and prey, no honor. I don't know what was going through that bison's head, and I don't know what was in Buddy Clement's. I don't know whether that seventeen-year-old maybe whispered a prayer under his breath as he and his family spent the day dressing the kill. But I know that to me then, the girl who couldn't hook a fish or look a steer in the face while she ate a steak, the whole thing seemed too easy to be respectful to the great sacrifice the animal had made.

The people of Montana weren't convinced it was possible for an outsider to fully understand the bison. I'd never run a cattle ranch, never been worried that a wild bison would infect my calves with brucellosis. I'd never seen a fence trampled by a stampede, or a tourist gored by a bull. A friend told me once that you're not considered a "native" in Montana unless your

grandparents were born there. Too many transplants were relo-
cating from California and New York and Oregon—with their
ski-out condos and their Nature Conservancy buying up land
to protect the remaining wild species—who didn't have the
context required to make these kinds of judgments. Without
the short memory of history—without grandparents' stories
of the days of frontier hardship and struggle—I couldn't know
what it was like to be afraid of a wild thing. I couldn't share the
desire to wrestle nature into submission.

But I did love bison. When I think of Montana now, my
memories of bison are among the strongest, my favorite.
Throughout that first year, I would take long wandering drives
alone, intentionally losing myself on winding mountain roads,
longing for discovery. Just a few miles south along the Galla-
tin River from Kevin's house was a small unmarked turnoff,
a dirt road that wound around the Flying D Ranch, owned by
Ted Turner. Turner established the ranch specifically for wildlife protection, and it's now home to established populations
of deer, elk, wolves, and bison. The Turner bison herd is nearly
five thousand strong, a greater population even than in nearby
Yellowstone.[4] I remember sitting in my car at the Flying D,
watching three or four bison lolling in the dry dead grass, one
wallowing against a small rise in the land, his massive head
slowly swinging back and forth as he scratched an itch against
the ground.

AFTER AWHILE, I started to feel antsy in Bozeman. I'm still
not sure why—maybe because I moved there to be closer to
Kevin, it never quite felt like a place that could belong to me.
Maybe Montana was all expectation for me, and the reality of
feeling like such an outsider, the lack of connection to a larger

community, left me wanting. Maybe my love of the historical frontier, enamored as I was by the awkward, lumpy-furred
bison, was just wanderlust, an overly romanticized crush on
cowboy culture, a wannabe road trip pipe dream with none
of the messiness of reality and daily life. Maybe it's Kerouac's
fault. Maybe the West is the place young people like me are
supposed to idealize: wild and unsettled and far from my East
Coast childhood.

Whatever the cause, I kept trying to change my life in Montana, kept trying to find a better way to fit. After just a few
months, I quit my job at the animal shelter, thinking that if I
had more free time to write, more creative energy to devote
to my own work, I might be happy. So I took a job as a nanny.
Years of high school babysitting experience made the search
easy, and I spent the next year and a half caring for someone
else's children.

The decision was practical, not sentimental. I did not antic-
ipate the tenderness, the new desires it opened in me. I spent
the mornings at home with a seven-month-old baby. Mostly, I
held him and fed him. Each morning, I felt the delicate pull of
devotion as he fell asleep in my arms. I sat above him, watching
his eyelids flicker, tiny muscles beneath soft pink flesh twitching in resistance to the slow sink of sleep. The bottle in his
mouth would fall still, a slight film of formula in the corners of
his mouth. I held his warm body like this every day, twice a day,
for nearly a year, watching him descend into thick milky sleep,
my heart straining with the ache of his little hands grabbing at
my shirt. I held him snugly but the bottle gently, able to pull
it from the suck of his mouth the moment he dropped asleep.

Being a nanny is a pseudo-motherhood. I ran the house, rins-
ing the lunchtime dishes and planning elaborate outings to the

science museum, taking neighborhood walks to feed the pond geese, orchestrating craft projects, and moderating childhood disputes. But the foremost duty, the one for which I was truly hired, the one that enabled me to feel closest to the baby and his six-year-old brother, was the responsibility of feeding them.

This wonderful dependence. A reason. The knowledge that they would be lost without me: beautiful and dangerous.

THE AUTUMN I moved to Montana, my mother also moved, her plane taking her towards nine months as a volunteer for a teacher training college in rural central Ghana. This was a natural extension of her life spent in the service of others—to her children and family, to the deaf and developmentally disabled students she began her career working with, to the eighth graders she taught Shakespeare, the grade no one else wanted. Now, to strangers in need of a resource room in a country where she knew no one. Whenever I thought of her during my first fall in Montana, my heart swelled with pride, to think of her indefatigable desire to care for others, her sense of purpose.

But when I thought of my father, home alone in New Hampshire, making pots of spaghetti by himself, ordering pizza for one, watching ESPN with dinner every night...I couldn't think about it too much. The image of him alone gave way to dangerous impulses. Little cracks formed in my chest, a desire to scrap my own plans, to abandon the career as a writer I'd planned to have in Montana, to move back in with my dad and cook for him until my mother came home.

Despite how hard I'd worked to distance myself from the kitchen-women of my family, I found myself occupying the position often: daily, I held a bottle to an infant's lips; nightly, I whispered, "I'll take care of dinner," like a declaration of love, to ease Kevin's burden. When I imagined the blue light of the television cast on my father eating alone, I felt heavy with the weight of caretaking. I wanted to take care of these men—and it scared me that I wanted to. The desire to nurture was inescapable, and it made me crazy, like a trapped wild animal. Every step a half step towards domesticity. I felt awkward. I started, like a deer sensing vulnerability. I was afraid of this desire, afraid to give too much of myself to caring for others. But there it was, in my blood: love as food. ·

ONE NIGHT THAT first year in Montana, Kevin and I had a big argument. He was having an especially busy time at school and I said something about feeling neglected. He told me he wished I hadn't moved to Montana, that having me there, needing attention, was too much of a burden. In a flare of anger, I stormed out and went out driving. I headed to the outskirts of town, on dark roads I didn't know well—I decided I would try to find a hidden hot spring we'd heard about and had been looking for together. I wanted to prove my independence, to reassert some ownership over this new state that I'd declared my home, to claim something separate from him. I wanted to find the hot springs first, to beat him there.

A yellow moon hung low in the sky when I set out, stopping to throw my bathing suit and a six-pack of Sam Adams—the beer that reminds me of home—in the back seat. I drove my first car, the one I'd just bought from my boss for $500 cash, a 1983 Toyota Camry hatchback nicknamed Dimples for the small pings and pocks littering the hood and roof, from the great Billings hailstorm of 1987. I barely even cared where I was headed. I just circled on the outskirts of town, muttering to myself.

I never found the hot springs that night; instead, I stopped the car on the side of a dark road with no buildings or headlights in sight, with only the faint silhouette of mountains visible, black against the navy sky. I drank a Boston Lager and fumed. After awhile, I realized I was angry because there was a small truth in what Kevin had said: I didn't have a purpose in Montana other than him. I had left the city and come west to find something, to find a connection and a community, to belong and be invested, but I still didn't quite know what I was looking for. I suddenly understood how much pressure that was, to pack everything I owned into two suitcases, present myself to someone else, and say, "What should I do now?"

I knew I was searching for clues in the wilderness, a guidebook to belonging. But where was the legend? What was the secret? What was I after when I made Kevin bring all of his environmental guidebooks along on our day hikes into the Spanish Peaks? Pointing and identifying: *What's that flower? What animal made this print? What's the bird that makes this sound?* When I studied the stories of bison hunts, grazing my fingers across sepia-toned photographs reprinted in books in the library section labeled *Frontier*?

Michael Perry has written that the land, the physical geography of a place, always welcomes you. But community, he says, is another story. You can't force your way in with the people.[5] Perhaps I connected only to the land of Montana, with the American bison and the Bridger Mountains, without ever really understanding the people who rooted themselves there, a people who fiercely defended their land, even as I saw it being trampled. Perhaps I was living in a perpetual state of cognitive dissonance: I thought of the hunt as a noble ritual, but I didn't want to see the blood and the struggle; I loved taking care of the people I loved, but I resented them for it; I loved the place, but I couldn't find anything to keep me grounded there.

I don't remember how Kevin and I resolved that fight, or if we even did. These memories exist, I know, but feel like such a distant part of my life. I remember days spent on the second-story balcony at the co-op, sitting on rough-hewn rails and benches, eating fake tuna sandwiches with Kevin and the boy I nannied, feeling like a family. I remember the beginning of our time there together, hiking into valleys and around lakes, our red cheeks and ears poking out from beneath woolen hats. I remember the view of snowy mountain peaks from the back-yard of the house I eventually shared with him, the evening sun setting behind them. Mostly, I remember nights like this one, with the fight and the failed search for the hot springs, nights spent alone and outside, wondering whether I belonged. I remember stretching back on the hail-pocked hood of my car, staring at the millions of distant stars, trying hard to locate the scent of sulfur.

A year and a half after I moved to Montana, I'd done little more than bounce between jobs and play at making a home. Gift shop girl, nonprofit development officer, nanny—unable to make a living as a creative writer, unable to write creatively while making a living. I focused instead on Kevin and our rela-tionship, constructing a life together with the scraps of our early twenties and little else. We drank vodka from Nalgene water bottles and swung ourselves around barefoot to blue-grass music in summer park festivals; we strapped on life vests and braved the Kitchen Sink rapids in the Madison River. I told myself a writer has to live to write, to gather material, but the truth is, I never had the connection to anything deeper required to write well, never had the roots or the safety of connectedness necessary for insight.

My toes were in the dirt, but this still wasn't enough to settle me into the place. I was always hyperconscious and sensitive to being ostracized, aware that I was not a native here. When Kevin finished college in December, he found a job with the National Park Service in Southern California, with a start date less than two weeks after his interview. He found a room for rent on Craigslist, packed the trunk of his Subaru, and moved to the beach. The matter of where I would live—whether I would stay in Montana and wait for his inevitable return or join him in California—was left up to me. I had nothing to lose.

Chapter Six

Strawberry Fields

I **WAS TWENTY-FOUR AND** everything I owned, including my bike, fit into the back of my 1983 Toyota Camry. I left Montana the same way I had D.C.—quickly, deciding it wasn't a fit and cutting my losses. I drove through Idaho and Utah, mountains still mostly covered with snow, leaving behind any lessons about community and belonging and understanding the frontier might have had to teach me. I entered scorching-hot desert landscapes in Arizona and Nevada, readying myself for a better world, a world already built for someone like me. Somewhere in the Mojave Desert, I pulled over at a rest stop to dig out the deeply buried sunscreen from a suitcase in the back of the car, but it was too late. I arrived in Ventura tired and sweaty, my left arm sunburned lobster red, as if I'd arrived after a long pilgrimage to the promised land.

The terrace of our first apartment in California faced east. Just outside the cement wall encasing the patio, grew a lemon tree. On my first morning there, in April 2007, I woke up to air crisp and cool like a September in the mountains, bright sun streaking through the window between giant ferns. A hummingbird flitted among birds-of-paradise. The sun caught the dew that had formed in the night on a dazzling yellow orb, which I picked, squeezing it fresh into my morning mug of green tea.

A fresh start, I thought. Here, in California, I would live as a writer. Here, in California, I would belong.

Just a few weeks earlier, I had deboarded the small plane at Oxnard Airport for an exploratory visit, wearing long linen pants and sandals, though the Southern California air still carried a bite. Kevin drove me straight to the Pacific Ocean, where I shed my sandals in the parking lot and walked across cool sand straight into the water. Icy, gray, clear. I inhaled deeply, remembering the smell of salt.

Hours later, we walked arm in arm down Ventura's Main Street and discovered a coffee shop in an alley laced with bougainvillea.

I said, "I already feel this is home."

Three weeks later, I moved south for good.

I BEGAN TO feed myself. Every Saturday, I could walk five blocks to the downtown farmers market—one of three markets in town each week—spend twenty dollars, and return with a backpack full of fresh produce. Meals consisted mostly of platters of simple washed vegetables, a few slices of baguette, some cheese, maybe a handful of nuts. I would chop and slice and occasionally fry in a little olive oil and garlic, but the fresh ingredients barely needed any attention. I'd sit outside with no shoes, inhaling the delicate sour of the lemon tree, and eat with my bare hands, asparagus spears drizzled with balsamic vinegar,

C-slices of mellow green avocado, salted tomato wedges, whole strawberries. I let the raw juices trickle between my fingers and licked daintily at the bone on the edge of my wrist, relishing.

California was a strange dreamworld, where seasons seemed to have no bearing. A California native will tell you the weather varies from November to June, but to us outsiders, those who have felt pangs in our shoulders from shoveling three feet of snow after a mid-April blizzard, who never lived with the possibility of Thanksgiving at the beach, the climate of southern coastal California is idyllic. Flawless. Perfect for growing.

Everything felt good and fresh and new. In my first week in Ventura, I landed a full-time job at an after-school tutoring center and a regular freelancing gig for a local arts weekly. I taught reading and wrote for a living. Perhaps more importantly, I met friends immediately who shared these interests. My coworkers read Gabriel García Márquez and listened to Ben Harper and had served in the Peace Corps. Kevin and I found a new apartment, three blocks from the ocean. I spent my days wandering in the sand, marveling at the water and typing at coffee shops with free wireless. I made barely $1,000 a month. I was twenty-four and lived at the beach. *This*, I thought, *was the life I imagined*—bright and warm and free, somehow more open with possibility and more alive with connection.

A COOL GRAY June day. I stood on a beach in Malibu beside a man named Mati Waiya as he told me the Chumash migration legend.

"The Creator built a Rainbow Bridge from the Channel Islands to the mainland, to guide the Chumash to their new home. He warned them not to look down into the sea during the crossing, but some could not resist the lure, and when they peered down over the edge of the Rainbow Bridge, they fell into the sea. Though they had disobeyed him, the Creator couldn't bear to watch his children die. Rather than allow them to drown, He transformed them into dolphins."

"The ocean," he said, "is more than a source of food for our people. It is the home of our ancestors."

Two months into my California summer, my editor had given me this feature assignment for the monthly local lifestyle magazine. Mati Waiya had recently been named the Ventura Coastkeeper, the first Native American to hold a position as part of the Waterkeeper Alliance, a coalition of non-profits dedicated to protecting and preserving global waterways.[1] He organized local volunteers and scientists to protect Ventura County's waterways by monitoring water quality, prosecuting polluters, and holding educational programs. Waiya had asked me to meet him at Nicholas Canyon Beach to show me the Chumash discovery village his foundation had constructed there, to explain the connection between his tribe's land ethic and his new responsibilities to the ocean.

When we wandered across the road to the bare strip of beach leading up to the ocean, the sky was heavy, wet, pocked with gulls. I asked Waiya what his organization's biggest issues were—the most serious threats to the waterways that were his to safeguard. He told me agriculture. I must have looked puzzled, because he asked me, "You don't know about the strawberries?"

Waiya described lush, plump strawberries as if they were a miracle, his large hands in the air in front of our faces plucking a ripe crop. He shook his head, long braid waving behind him, as he described the people who walked between the strawberry rows using backpack sprayers to fumigate the crops with methyl bromide. The synthetic fertilizers and the residual pesticide toxins ran off the soil here in heavy rains, the storm water drifting into streams and rivers and eventually the ocean. Ventura County, he told me, ranked fourth in the state—the biggest agricultural producer in the country—for its use of these chemicals, which he called "agritoxins." Eventually, the chemicals found their way into the bodies of fish, into the drinking water, worming back up the food chain, poisoning land and people. They were linked to cancer and other dangerous side effect words: "immunotoxicity," "neurological impairment," "fauna morphology."

The chemicals weren't only found in the area's food, which was sold all over the country. The people most at risk were those handling the backpack sprayers full of chemicals, the farmworkers, mostly immigrants and migrant workers. Cancer rates in California were highest among members of the United Farm Workers. And their children—the children of farmworkers—had much higher risks of cancers and developmental disorders.

I scribbled furiously, stunned. Five pages of my reporter's notebook filled with strawberries. At home that night, I searched the Internet for more information, for the research to support Waiya's description of strawberries, to develop this article. I planned to expand my profile into a feature, an exposé of the poisons of California's agriculture and how they affected the migrant populations most. Instead, I found an investigative piece by journalist Eric Schlosser—"In the Strawberry Fields," originally published in 1994.[2]

This was known. This was general knowledge. I couldn't believe it. I couldn't believe that as someone who cared deeply about ethical food, and someone who had spent the better part of her twenties identifying herself as an activist, I had never read this story. I didn't understand why it hadn't come across my radar. I couldn't believe how easy it still was for me to be surprised by some new offense, some inhumanity to be excavated. I marveled, not for the first time, at the deep, dark blindness that my middle-class privilege afforded me.

I read Schlosser's lengthy article that night, and then more and more in the weeks to follow, following links and references to learn all I could about labor in the agriculture industry.

I learned that, because of its gorgeous weather, California had been the country's number one food and agricultural producer for decades.[3] More than half of the fruits, nuts, and vegetables sold in the United States are grown in California, which is also the number one dairy state. More than 70 percent of the country's olives, and more than 80 percent of its strawberries, come from California. Almonds, artichokes, dates, figs, and kiwis are grown only in California.

California's unique climate is, in other words, the reason why most of us have developed a taste for strawberries in January or avocado in March.

But sheer volume of production itself was not entirely the problem. The problem was the experience of actually working on a farm. According to the California Institute for Rural Studies, the typical farmworker in the U.S. is a young man who has left his family to work in the field.[4] He usually spends between twelve and fourteen hours a day in the field, six days a week, and makes between $7,000 and $10,000 a year. The farmworker has no health insurance. No sick days, no vacation days, and certainly no union. More than 50 percent have never been to a dentist; about one third have never seen a doctor. Typically, farms provide housing for their workers during the growing and harvesting season, to maximize the picking hours in a day. Workers can expect to pay about $50 a week to live in rundown shacks or trailers, sometimes with as many as fifteen other people.

Farmworkers get all of this in exchange for picking the food we need, for working what I discovered was the third most dangerous job in the country. The odds of dying on the farm are 39 out of 100,000. Farmworkers suffer the highest rate of toxic chemical injuries and skin disorders of any workers in the country, and are more than 25 percent more likely than the average American to develop asthma, birth defects, tuberculosis, and cancer.

Children of migrant farmworkers have higher rates of pesticide exposure, dental disease, and malnutrition. This isn't, I learned, only because they live in close proximity to the farm. It's because the agricultural industry is exempt from the Fair Labor Standards Act's child labor regulations. The minimum age to work legally in any other industry in this country is sixteen. On the farm, it's twelve.

I wasn't entirely surprised to learn that the vast majority of California's farmworkers—and, in fact, a majority of farmworkers across the country—are undocumented immigrants. I knew, abstractly, that migrant workers picked our food. I'd just never really thought about what that meant: that more than 50 percent of migrant farmworkers nationwide are not protected by legal documents and so, in this country, have no legal rights. There is no safety net to protect them, and very little sympathy in the American consciousness. This lack of documentation, along with a tight bottom line and a slim margin of economic error, adds up to truly horrible working conditions on the modern American corporate farm.

A COMMON REFRAIN heard when Americans discuss migrant farmworkers is the notion of choice: if you don't like it, don't do it. So why do they? If it's so backbreaking, hot, exhausting, dangerous, and underpaid, why would anyone sign up to work on these farms? Because they don't have any other option, of course.

When sociologists discuss patterns of migration, they have two terms to explain what makes a person move from one place to the next—"push factors" and "pull factors." It's easy to deduce that what draws migrants to this work is the danger of the U.S. agricultural industry. Because the jobs are so life threatening, employers would have to raise pay and improve conditions to get working-class Americans interested. Instead, the industry recruits workers from abroad, where there are more laborers, fewer jobs, and much, much lower wages, pulling them across the border. The U.S. agricultural industry is located primarily in California, where a cheap and willing supply of labor is close at hand. Why provide health care and housing when you can just import migrants instead?

The push factors are the things that make a person's home country worth leaving behind. Let's put it this way: the push factors are the things that make working eighty-hour weeks hunched over in a field under the blazing sun for seven grand a year look like the American dream come true. It's got to be pretty bad where you're living if that's your idea of opportunity.

Before you begin to think that the solution here is to close the borders and take those jobs back, I should make it clear that this is a pretty good deal for the American consumers, too. Paying migrant farmworkers next to nothing and having a constant stream of people willing to work cheap is what keeps us all in fresh produce, year round, for pennies. It's the reason why

I can walk into a grocery chain in the middle of February and buy a head of lettuce for ninety-nine cents. And if the cheap food itself weren't benefit enough, the U.S. Social Security Administration has recently estimated that three out of every four undocumented immigrants pay payroll taxes (in addition to paying the same sales and consumer taxes the rest of us pay), and that undocumented workers contribute $6 billion to $7 billion dollars in social security funds that they are not eligible to claim.

Plus, show me the pools of American citizens out there just dying for a job picking lettuce in Oxnard.

The size and scope of this exploitation overwhelmed me, as, once again, I was forced to realize just how little I really knew about food. When I sat in Professor Bob's classroom and watched how livestock animals were treated in factory farms, I was horrified. But even produce farms, I was learning, were awful, abusive places. Perhaps the worst part of discovering how exploitative farms could be was having to face the fact that I'd learned about animals before I'd learned about people. In no abstract or uncertain terms, this meant the national dialogue about the food industry cared more about cattle than about human beings.

I still cared, deeply, about the helpless, trapped animals being harmed and slaughtered by factory farms, but I was staggered by disappointment—mostly at myself. How could I not have known this? How could it never have even occurred to me to look?

IF YOU TAKE a left down Telephone Road in Ventura and drive to the end, you'll hit the T-junction at Olivas Park Drive—always my favorite road there. Stretching for ten miles clear across the city, from the beach into the suburbs of Oxnard, the road was then relatively undeveloped, lined on both sides by spacious agricultural fields.

And right at that T-junction, in a little red barn converted into a small market, the owner of this property sold produce straight off the field all week long. The floor was cement, the aisles constructed out of plastic folding tables stacked with wooden crates holding small piles of fruits and vegetables. I'd usually stop on my way home from work, grab a head of red Bibb lettuce or a pint of berries, a couple of oranges, just to run my fingers over this, the freshest food I could imagine.

I would carry my purchases from the Olivas Park market to a cooler in the back seat, then drive to the beach to read or write for an hour while I watched the sun set. And when I drove away from the market, I would smile at the workers I saw out in the fields, proud to be able to watch the rhythm of their work, bending and standing, over and over, tossing watermelons down a line of brown hands.

I don't know that the workers in those fields were badly treated. I don't know what they were paid, or where they lived, or what language they spoke. I'm not even opposed to migrant workers picking my food, so long as they receive a living wage. But the unsafe conditions, the pollution, all of it was right there for me to see, and I'd spent nearly five years as a vegetarian, thinking I was doing some good. I'd spent the summer reveling in California: riding my bike to the beach, watching the Perseid meteor shower while soaking in a natural hot spring, carrying produce home from the farmers market in my hemp backpack, feeling proud and entitled and alive. But I'd been willfully naïve, wanting so badly for the ethical life to be cheap and easy and accessible. This—the conditions of life on the farm—was a story I, the ethical vegetarian, should have known. This was my agricultural paradise.

IN DOWNTOWN VENTURA stands a beautiful pier, a teetering wooden relic stretching 1,600 feet out over the ocean from the mainland. I visited often to sit and smell the salt water and feel the sticky sea breeze tangle my hair. Fishing off the end of the pier is allowed, so the stench of fish guts has sunk into the wood, its wide, thick planks sticky and wet with blood, and with the ocean. Salt water sprays the pier constantly, embedding sharp crystals and dank, faint rot into the meat of the wood. I sat on the pier and watched days pass, immersed in sea, in the loud caws of gulls circling like buzzards, the spray stinging my porous skin, the hot sun sizzling my burning shoulders. New patterns emerged. Who got to eat the food of the paradise I'd thought I lived in. And how. The stink of fish everywhere.

Some, I saw, fished for fun. White and Chicano families gathered around one or two poles, a red plastic cooler with long necks and juice boxes, a portable stereo hissing a crackling connection from the mainland, a picnic of ziplocked bologna and cheese sandwiches, peanut butter and jelly on white bread, baggies of grapes. The fathers wrapped their arms around children, guiding the long thin line down into the sea. They threw fish bodies onto ice or the plastic cutting boards nailed to some of the pier's benches. They laughed.

Some fished without laughing. These are the men—mostly men, almost always men—I saw sitting cross-legged on sidewalks outside the Main Street Ben & Jerry's or curled, sleeping, surrounded by garbage bags beneath the trees in Fir Street Park. Men who walked more slowly than any others I'd seen,

not because they were laden with all their worldly posses-
sions, though they were—wearing flannels tied around their
waist, leading scrappy matted dogs on leashes of rope, pushing
rusty bicycles sagging with the weight of accumulation—but
because they had nowhere to be. These men fished off the pier
with scrabbled-together equipment, with branches—actual
tree branches, stripped of foliage—and worms not purchased
from the small tackle stand at Fifth and Laurel but dug from
the ground or gathered, after rain, in discarded Chinese takeout
containers.

There seemed to be more homeless people in Ventura than
anywhere else I'd lived. I chalked it up to summer, and living
near the ocean, in the crook of California's coast that stays tem-
perate year round. The public space in Ventura is shared, so I
spent time in parks and beaches and on the promenade, where
the homeless, too, set up their makeshift camps. When I lived
in vibrant Washington, D.C., by contrast, the homeless lived
elsewhere, in rougher neighborhoods where upper-middle-
class college graduates doing nonprofit work were unlikely to
wander.

Over the course of the summer, as I watched the homeless
fishing side by side with young fathers and children on the
pier, as I learned about the intersections of food and choice, as
I discovered all that I had been privileged enough not to have
to see, I began to wonder what else I was missing. I began to
wonder whether the availability of food played any role in the
congregation of the homeless in this beach city. In addition to
the large number of homeless people, the nonprofit organization California Food Policy Advocates estimates that about
47 percent of adults in Ventura County live in food insecure
households, where a lack of resources disrupts eating patterns.[5]

Maybe, I realized, the homeless came to the ocean for something to eat.

Fish bodies piled and glistened in the midday sun, the wet of the ocean evaporating with a slight buzz in the heat. Men with meaty hands wrestled the fish dead, the left hand wrapped around the body, holding it still, while the right hand delivered a blow with the handle of a knife to the back of the fish's head. The tail was removed, thrown back to the ocean. Blades wriggled between skin and muscle, peeling back the shimmering silver scales. The men with families used their wrists to lift baseball caps slightly and tossed the fish bodies into a cooler, onto ice, for dinner back at home, panfried and seasoned with lemon, or grilled in aluminum-foil packets over a low charcoal burn, served with grilled corn, a citrus salad.

The men with their dogs and their bicycles, they tossed the fish, whole, into white plastic buckets, mucked around the edges. Later in the night, I could see them in small packs on the beach, gathered like hunched birds around a fire in the sand, fish impaled on sticks, held over an open flame. There, in the dark, I heard their rough, distant laughter, saw the bottles wrapped in brown paper, smelled the burning flesh of the unskinned fish.

ONCE, ON A street in Ventura, a homeless man asked me to buy his pregnant wife a meal. I hear, now, how it sounds like a scam, sounds like something you'd say to a twenty-four-year-old girl with a laptop in her arms, wearing flip-flops at noon on a weekday. But this middle-aged balding man in a stained white tank top walked up to me and said, "Excuse me, miss?" He told me he wasn't going to ask me for money, so I wouldn't think he was going to waste it on booze. He told me they'd just been evicted, and his wife was six months pregnant and having crav- ings. All she wanted in the world right now was eggs Benedict from the Busy Bee Cafe. Something in his "Excuse me" broke my heart. I chose to believe him.

But when I walked into the Busy Bee, they didn't have eggs Benedict on the menu. I panicked. I wasn't going back out to that man to say his wife couldn't have the one thing she wanted to eat, so I flagged down a waitress and begged. I begged her and she special-ordered two eggs Benedict for me. I paid the $14.50 and brought them back out to the man, who had pointed to his dirty shirt when he told me he'd just wait out- side, who started to cry when I said I'd gotten one for him, too.

When we were kids on family vacation, my parents always took our restaurant leftovers in doggie bags, even when we were staying at a hotel without a refrigerator, or leaving the next morning. We'd find a nearby park and leave the leftovers still packaged in their nondescript plastic bags on a bench somewhere in plain sight next to a trash can. My parents wanted to teach us nothing should go to waste in a world with so much need.

When I left the man in Ventura in front of the Busy Bee Cafe, I barely made it around the corner before I slumped against the warm brick of a Main Street building, tears all over my face. Not because, or not only because, I had looked straight at the face of need. But because even if he had been lying—even if they hadn't been evicted, or his wife wasn't pregnant, or he didn't have a wife, or they were addicts, even if any of those worst- case stereotypes were true—what was he going to do with eggs Benedict besides eat them? Even if he had lied, he had told the lie just so that he could have something he really *wanted* to eat.

Again, the national conversation is one of choice: the

assumption is that if you don't have enough, whether because you're homeless or jobless or an underpaid worker in subpar housing, it's because that's the life you've chosen. You've picked it for yourself—by being a drug addict or an immigrant, by having a mental illness or not speaking English.

I had never wanted to be, had never thought of myself as, the kind of person who subscribes to those myths. I know poverty and addiction and mental illness are not choices, and that thinking of the homeless or undocumented as somehow deserving of that life is just a way of further distancing ourselves from the possibility of ever falling down our own rabbit holes of despair or loss.

But California was showing me that privilege means not having to see the cracks—the massive gaps where whole segments of society get swallowed up. I walked to the farmers market and the beach, I marveled at the fresh produce and smiled at the quaint fishing, and I never thought about where it came from, or who wasn't lucky enough to access it.

At the end of the Ventura pier, there is a warning sign about the kinds of fish you can catch there, about which ones are safe for children and pregnant women to eat. The sign, posted by the California Office of Environmental Health Hazard Assessment advises against eating certain species from certain locations and recommends that all other fish be thoroughly skinned before consumption to avoid any risk of contamination. Some species are too dangerous, their fatty tissues deposits of high-dose toxic chemicals, the ones that Mati Waiya taught me leech into the waterways from those abundant strawberry fields.

I might have been able to scrub clean the vegetables I bought at the market to avoid pesticides, but the workers spraying the fields couldn't avoid the toxins. *I* might have been able to choose what kind of food I wanted to eat—what, as a vegetarian, was humane or safe. I chose to eat based on a sense of purpose. But how easy it is to assume choice is equally available. Not everyone gets that choice.

The happy families on the pier can afford to choose: they laugh and reel in their fish, and sometimes toss them back. They examine the fish bodies for fungus or other evidence of internal decay, and if the fish look bad, if they are of the wrong species, they throw the contaminated food back into the ocean, and reach into the cooler for a Fruit Roll-Up.

The men with bicycles and trash bags—I don't think they ever throw a fish back.

Chapter Seven

Chickpeas for Breakfast

M Y THIRD MORNING in Ghana, in 2007, my mother and I emerged from the guest bedroom we were sharing, hair wet from the shower, skin already beginning to bead with moisture in the heavy July heat of West Africa. We padded across the bare concrete floor of the living room. No one else was yet seated behind the dressing screen folded around the card table that designated the dining area, but we knew they had been awake for hours, performing chores in the 3:00 AM dark while we huddled beneath our mosquito nets and tried to ignore the rooster calls. We sat and waited at the table for our hosts to join us. A flat yellow pancake of egg substitute waited on my plate. Two cans stood side by side on the table: an open can of thick, sweet evaporated milk and an unopened can of chickpeas.

Here, in rural Bechem, five hours on a pocked red-dirt road inland from the capital city of Accra, my mother had spent a year living as a volunteer, working to build a resource center at

St. Joseph College of Education, the city's small teacher training university. When my mother finished her volunteer stint the year before, she had vowed to return and visit what she now thought of as an extension of her family. This time, I joined her for a two-week visit.

My mother knew her eldest daughter well, knew that I would jump at the chance to travel so far from my suburban upbringing, would thrive on the exposure and opportunity. She couldn't have known what the timing meant to me, that at that moment, in the middle of my summer in California, I was again looking for purpose. After several years struggling to find my community as an ethical vegetarian, I thought I'd settled into a home, and a healthy food system, in California. But now I saw how many people were left out of that system, and I didn't know how to make sense of that. How I'd misplaced the sense of radical commitment to an ethical way of life that had dictated my dietary choices. How I'd ended up on the wrong side, part of a community but blinded by privilege to the questions of access. I was eager, that summer, for a reminder of why I wanted to live ethically, responsibly. I was eager to get back to work.

Mr. Mensah soon joined us at the breakfast table. He was the man who had been my mother's boss for a year, the principal of the teacher training college. The two of them had worked together to bring two computers into the resource center, to teach the students how to use the Internet, to make lesson-planning handouts and organize workshops to help send his students out into the smaller villages as skilled teachers. A dignified man but soft-spoken, he wore a royal-blue gown draped richly across the dark skin of his arm.

"Oh," he said, picking up the unopened can of chickpeas and leaving the room.

I felt a wave of relief—I hate chickpeas. They crumble too softly and easily between my teeth, like chewing sticky pads of dirt, like flavorless peanut butter stuck in a thick paste against the roof of my mouth. The idea of eating them, gritty and cold, for breakfast, made my already sensitive stomach turn.

I heard the screen door that led towards Adjoa's outdoor kitchen creak open and slam behind Mr. Mensah, and his distant voice calling, staccato, "Mother."

Soon, he returned, open can of slimy beige beans waiting in hand. He lowered the can, graciously, directly in front of me on the table.

"Adjoa is worried about you," he said. "You need protein."

WHEN I BECAME a vegetarian, five years earlier, my mother had insisted I see a nutritionist. She was worried about my protein, too. I assured her I had done my reading. I learned which nutrients came primarily from meat (iron, protein, omega-3 fatty acids, vitamin B12) and how to replace them. I knew that with a healthy focus on nuts and vegetables, there was little danger of a protein deficiency. I also knew that modern Americans drastically over-consumed meat, and I knew the result: surging world-record rates of heart disease and obesity. I knew I didn't want to buy into the myth of meat consumption. What I said to my mother, to convince her of my health and safety, and to others who challenged me in the years that followed was that although meat had played an important role in the biological development of humans, in our modern world, with the options for alternative protein sources now available, humans did not *need* to eat meat to survive.

What I learned in Ghana was that nothing is so simple.

I was lucky, on this trip to Africa, that I was not a complete stranger. My dietary adjustments were not as big a hurdle as they would have been if I had traveled alone, since my mother could explain in advance that her whiter-than-a-beluga daughter did not, in fact, eat meat. Voluntarily. And Adjoa, the matriarch of the Mensah family, had accommodated me generously. For the two weeks I stayed in their enormous-by-Bechem-standards, one-story, two-bedroom house, she cooked me three meals a day without meat.

One night, she made her famous *pepe* soup, a watery broth the deep rust of an heirloom tomato, spiked with grated red chili pepper. This was neither the smoky burn of chipotle nor the clean wet heat of a jalapeño, and not the coarse cough-in-the-back-of-your-throat of black pepper. This was fire engine. This was nose-running, ears-sweating, hair-frizzling heat, the kind of heat that I felt under my skin like a sunburn, blood surging towards the surface. My lips tingled, nearly numb by the time I reached the bottom of the bowl.

As a picky vegetarian white girl from New England, this was a little outside my comfort zone. But so was Africa, and I craved discomfort. On this trip, I relished every obstacle, every unfamiliarity, everything I'd never tried, as a learning experience. This trip was the jolt of electricity I thought I needed, a way to reconnect with en ethical identity, a reminder of the value of paying attention to what's difficult to look at—poverty and inequality—a reminder to focus on the people behind the issues, their world, their lives. So I ate the entire blistering bowl of *pepe* soup like a rite of passage, a slap in the face of my complacency.

But as I lifted the heavy ceramic bowl to my mouth to swallow the last few drops, I saw faint gray flecks stuck like algae beneath the last dregs of broth: the remnants of the shredded goat that Adjoa had cooked in the *pepe* soup before serving it, careful to ladle my bowl full without any meat.

Although she never brought it up with me, I know Adjoa expressed surprise over my dietary choice to my mother—because meat, rare and expensive as it was, was a crucial part of her children's healthy diet. Without the very occasional animal meat they consumed, their diet would be largely absent of protein. And no amount of dried, boxed egg substitute, no can of chickpeas, nothing flown in by the United Nations in giant blue boxes would make up for that. When I discovered chevon, the goat meat in my *pepe* soup at Adjoa's table, I did not make a fuss. I did not remind her or my mother what being a vegetarian meant to me or why I had chosen to become one. For most of the two weeks I spent in Ghana, I did what I did that night: I sat back and watched. I was coming to terms with the limitations of what I thought I knew, the realization of pesticides and migrant laborers of California fresh in my mind. I decided to shut up and listen instead. To learn a world that in no way resembled the world I thought I lived in.

MOSTLY, THE PEOPLE of Bechem eat high-starch carbohydrates. Yam and cassava are the staple crops of a West African diet. One night, we had fried yams—not the yams of your Thanksgiving marshmallow casserole, not sweet potatoes, but massive beasts of a root vegetable, thin slices of dense white-yellow flesh fried in a homemade corn oil, a sort of Ghanaian french fry. When Adjoa pulled them from the red clay soil of her garden, the yams were fully the length of my arm and three times the width, enormous, elongated potatoes. She spent the entire afternoon scooping the flesh from the skin, mixing it aggressively with water in a big wooden bowl on the ground. Sitting on a small three-legged stool, she spun the bowl while her daughter-in-law pounded the yam flesh with a six-foot-long, flat-headed stick—fast, delicate hands barely missed by the insistent hammering. Only after all this, to remove the plant's natural toxins that would make it otherwise inedible, poisonous for humans, could the flesh be boiled. The glutinous flesh was shaped into flat chips, then fried, before making it to our table.

We ate peeled cassava root, again boiled for safe consumption, another tuber vegetable resembling the potato, the width of a banana, long and bumpy, curved in strange places. The thick tendril of the cassava was the first root vegetable I'd seen that actually resembled the gnarled twists of an ancient tree. A tougher, less flavorful potato, hard as a rock coming out of the earth, so heavy with starch it nearly forms a dough in your mouth as you chew it. This is what grows in Ghana.

We ate bananas—small, purple-green, sweet fruits, nothing like Chiquita—and plantains, pineapple, mango. We ate canned food, from milk to chickpeas to water chestnuts. Since neither the Mensahs nor the entire country of Ghana had a reliable source of electricity, we ate what was nonperishable or could be picked right before the meal.

On average, my mother told me, during her time there, the family ate meat about once a week—usually a chicken purchased on the way back from church and slaughtered for Sunday dinner. Occasionally, they would eat a can of pickled mackerel, or a spare side of beef or chevon traded at the market for Adjoa's bread, which she produced in mass quantities to sell.

About once a week. And the Mensahs were, by far, the wealthiest family in Bechem.

When I sat at the Mensahs' breakfast table, choking down cold, slimy chickpeas for breakfast, I marveled at how easy it was for me to decide to stop eating meat, and what an impossible decision it would have been for any of the residents of Bechem. I mashed up the beans with my fork, trying to mix them into the cold eggs to mask the taste and texture. How could I possibly have a conversation about why I chose not to eat meat with Adjoa, whose children have all been hospitalized for malaria? How was it possible that I hadn't, until now, seriously considered the reality that there are places in the world where food doesn't come so easy, a world without grocery home delivery or twenty-four-hour Walmarts or McDonald's drive-throughs?

TO SAY THERE is no public transportation in Ghana would be an understatement. For the most part, there is no transportation. The roads, what few there are, are rarely paved. This is usually a blessing. When pavement exists, it is so degraded—whole chunks of asphalt missing, large triangles split and moved off-center by traffic, creating dangerous rock outcrops in the middle of the road—that accidents often occur. On our one day-trip out of Bechem during my visit, Clement, one of the Mensahs' adult sons who had worked with my mother, took us to the slave castles at Cape Coast, but we got a flat tire that took three hours to fix. The tire iron bent in Clement's hands when he tried to wrench free the lug nuts, so we had to wait for passing motorists to stop and help. This took another hour of waiting, the fake flat tire being a common ruse used by roadside bands of robbers to attack good Samaritans.

Mostly, the people of Bechem get around town by walking. Water is available on the college campus, and the man who pulls the yellow cart at which cell phone minutes are sold usually parks right outside the gates, knowing his wealthiest customers live just inside. But getting anything else—food, books, paper, beer, clothes—means walking two miles into downtown Bechem.

This is not a difficult walk, excepting the more than one-hundred-degree temperatures, the flat dirt road not unlike the hard-packed mountain trails I've spent much of my life climbing for fun. Walking from St. Joseph's clear across Bechem, all the way to the cocoa plantation on the far eastern side of town is only a total of eight miles one way. But this is where the grocery store is, where the tailor who makes all the town's clothes works; it's the location of the only printer, only public phone, only bar. No bank, no post office.

One afternoon, my mother and I walked casually back across town from the cocoa plantation we'd toured, sweating in the red dust, chatting with a series of coming and going friends passing and recognizing her. I thought about how many times a day I go "into town" and back, thought about the option of stopping for a pint of berries or an organic red bell pepper on my way home from work. The things I took with me, the things I carried home, in my car and not on foot. Could this body carry me? What would happen to those errands if I were recovering from malaria? If I had a stomach virus from the water? If I had a child, or three? What would happen to my body if I went into town, on foot, carrying everything, once a day? The idea of *needing* protein began to look a little different.

St. Joseph's, where the Mensahs lived, provided an entire campus complex of houses and apartment buildings and shared gardening space for faculty, staff, and students. Within the crumbling concrete walls painted yellow, families lived communally, keeping small plots of land to grow bananas, mangos, or plantains, trading cultivated fruits for baked goods with neighbors, and raising small livestock operations.

While walking the pathways that wove across campus, I often encountered a roaming chicken, white feathers dusted with kicked-up red dirt. Once, a loping goat followed me all the way down the road to the mango tree, unabashedly munching the grass around me while I read. Her floppy gray ears swung in the hot air, swatting at dizzy flies.

Eating these animals was a rare occurrence for the families that raised them; selling their milk or eggs for months was more productive. When the animal was too old to be worth much of anything else and was slaughtered, the meat was sold. Livestock animals were for business, not for cooking. But these business models were clearly casual, not large scale. No feedlots or rows of battery cages, no artificial insemination or growth hormones or antibiotics. I saw a lot of poverty in Africa, big holes, chunks of absence like the disastrous pocks in the pavement, the comfort of a secure source of income broken and uprooted. But I didn't meet anybody with type 2 diabetes or the luxury of turning down a steak.

ON THE SIDES of the roads we whirred past as we drove from the capital city of Accra to Bechem, market stands sprung up in the most unlikely places. As I looked out the window at the blurs of African forest, a heavy near-jungle of dense low-slung greenery, looping vine-branches and scrappy underbrush, plywood tables would suddenly appear, two poles and a piece of cloth draped over them, a few scattered people selling bananas, papaya, cell phone minutes, meat.

These roadside stands were one of the only places to buy meat in Ghana, usually in the form of either giant snails or bushmeat. The giant snails, still in their shell, loomed the size of my spread hands, dirty tan-brown with black, slimy heads emerging from one end, piled high on a flat woven basket balanced on the head of a young man pacing the edges of the road, calling to customers.

And bushmeat. The mystery of the phrase still lingers. I've seen glimpses of the animal, far below the status to be eaten by the Mensah family—they would have been insulted if I'd asked whether they had ever eaten bushmeat. In my distant glances from passing cars, the bodies, dead and already skinned, draped over racks made of wooden poles, looked vaguely like large squirrels. Obscure brown animals with bushy reddish tails, the pink-white flesh of the body underneath all that remained. I have no idea what kinds of animals bushmeat came from. I asked multiple people multiple times, and I only ever got one answer: a shrug. It was just bushmeat.

WHEN I RETURNED from Ghana, everyone wanted to hear about it. I told them I was "still processing," but the truth is, I was avoiding talking about it, avoiding trying to figure out what I learned, or what it meant to me, because I didn't know. I didn't know what to say, where to begin, what would be patronizing, what would boggle the American mind most, or whether it was my right to do that. I fluctuated wildly between swells of rage and hope.

But I did feel something in Ghana, the familiar stirring in the pit of my stomach, the sensation of helplessness and rage in the face of injustice that combines to form activism. I remembered that I lived in a world of gross inequality but had only been paying attention to the mistreatment of animals. I didn't have my lip piercings anymore, and my hair had long since grown out from shaving it, and somewhere along the way I'd lost sight of that girl's values. I didn't know where my food came from in a deeper sense—who picked it or what it took, and who was lucky enough to eat it. I'd been so focused on appearing to be an agent of radical change that I wasn't really changing anything.

What I did know was that when I came back from Ghana, it was time to start writing again, in earnest. I knew that the people of Bechem reminded me of what's at stake in the choices we make about what food to eat.

I knew that the people who ate bushmeat were the ones who lived in the mud huts out in the forests, outside the limits of anything you could call a town.

I knew that on the southern coast, the number of fish caught by the villagers on any given day directly equaled the amount of food they had to eat that night.

I knew Adjoa was so worried about my protein intake she fed me chickpeas for breakfast.

A shift had occurred in me, from naïve idealist to realist. I knew thinking about food and making simple supermarket choices would no longer be enough. I knew real change would come from a willingness to accept complexity, and from a willingness to work.

IN *THE OMNIVORE'S DILEMMA*, Michael Pollan references the theological notion of table fellowship—the social bond created by the sharing of a meal—as one of his several arguments against vegetarianism, suggesting that choosing to abstain from meat for ethical reasons alienates an eater from the ability to fully form this bond. Focusing too intently on *what* we eat, instead of on *with whom*, means we miss out on something important.

My childhood, food rooted to family, made table fellowship an easy concept for me to understand. I had lived it. But it was in those moments around the Mensahs' dining table, choking down food that made me gag because my host wanted to take care of me, that I first fully grasped something important, that I first truly saw the chasm that could exist. The distance between how I wanted to eat and how they needed to. The truth that not everyone has the luxury of choosing their diet.

And, still, at the heart of all this, of everything, the table itself, and the love in the act of feeding.

I knew, too, that Adjoa would be embarrassed if she read this. She wouldn't say anything, but she loved her life. I couldn't speak when I returned from Africa because I couldn't— wouldn't—permit anyone to feel pity for the Mensahs. Because Adjoa didn't think of her family's food choices as scarce, or less than, or limited. Every single day, when she rolled out of bed at three in the morning to begin baking bread to sell on Saturday at the market, she slipped on her loose-fitting purple T-shirt and leggings. She walked silently out to her kitchen, straddled a bench and began mixing flour and water, kneading until her palms turned white. And while she worked the dough, palms flat against the tough gluten, she sang.

"Joy like a river, joy like a river, joy like a river in my soul."

Chapter Eight

Corn Fed

WALKING THROUGH A cornfield is a strange experience, a combination of natural retreat and industrial efficiency. Green floppy leaves brushed against my shoulder as I wriggled between the stalks, thick as my wrist and unbelievably straight, the rows so close together I could hardly make my way through. I learned later that corn is almost entirely machine planted and harvested now, so walking rows has become obsolete.

The previous autumn, shortly after I returned from my visit to Ghana, I'd perched on a small stone wall at Ventura Beach and watched the sun set into the Pacific Ocean, my toes curling around the cool, rough stones, a composition notebook in my hand, scribbling notes about why I wanted to go to graduate school for writing.

I wrote about my students at the tutoring center: the illiterate twenty-two-year-old nannies for Orange County lawyers, the five-year-olds who couldn't sit still long enough to listen in school, the brown-skinned high school quarterbacks who knew a scholarship was their only shot at affording college.

I wrote about Africa, what I saw there. I wrote about methyl bromide and strawberries.

I stared at the sunset and thought about food. Food as life force. Food as connection. But I also thought of food burdened by mistake. I thought of how I'd spent years so far as a vegetarian drifting, trying to make a difference but getting nowhere, hoping in the direction of purpose but never wrapping my hands around it. I'd left D.C. because I'd felt like an island floating alone in a city. I'd never found myself in Montana because I'd only seen what made me different. In California, I'd finally found a sense of place and self, only to have it upended by my own lack of awareness, my own privilege. Tired of wandering through the country alone, tired of so easily losing my way, tired of hoping and losing hope, I wanted to find a way to feed others and to feed myself. I wanted something right. Graduate school was my attempt to find a marriage. Could I finally find utopia, a world where I could believe in and work for change but not feel so alone?

I wrote a series of fragmented scenes for my application essay, stringing together the concrete-pounding purpose of D.C., the dramatic beauty of Montana, the connective force of Southern California, like a series of waves lapping the shore, quiet and persistent but moving closer, creeping up the beach. The tide was rising.

THIS WAS HOW I found myself, a year after I returned from Ghana, in Iowa. After a late-summer twilight drive, I'd found a cornfield out on a long stretch of road where I couldn't see a house. I was pretty sure walking around someone's cornfield would be considered trespassing, but I felt, as I often do, the need to come in close contact with the flora and fauna of a new place. I dipped my toes in the cold water of upstate New York's glacier-fed gorges. I hiked in the Bridger Mountains in Bozeman, picking wild flowers to identify and scouring the soil for bear tracks. I visited the Pacific Ocean and let kelp drape itself around my bare ankles in California. In Iowa, I figured, a cornfield was the iconic thing. Not because I couldn't find a prairie—I could, and had loved walking around, native grasses tickling my summer calves—but because there is more corn in Iowa than anything else, more than woods or prairie, more than roads or houses or people. This was the defining characteristic of my new hometown, and I'd never seen a corn plant up close before.

I didn't make it very far into the cornfield, but I was far enough to be completely submerged in corn, my orange sneakers dusted with dirt, my shoulders pulled forward in front of my body, proud, straight corn extending well over my head. I stared up at the fading purple sky through silky threads and watched distant stars begin to appear. Each time a car rushed by out on the road, a residual breeze rustled the leaves of the plants around me into a soft whisper. I scuffed my toes into the dirt beneath my feet, turning heavy clumps of black soil.

I'd met many farmers' sons and daughters in my classes over the course of the last year. When I looked at them, with their pickup trucks and John Deere hats, when they spoke to each other about their family's century farms, I heard a deep abiding commitment that neither natural disaster nor bankruptcy could sever. Agriculture was a way of life here, passed down through generations. Their families felt a connection to the land different from the one I had developed as a suburban child, to the small patch of woods behind my house. The land was their livelihood, their home, their community, and their identity. A beautiful relationship to a plot of ground.

But when I stood in the cornfield, I couldn't conjure that sense of connection for myself. I was removed, distant, despite the suffocating closeness of the stalks. I wasn't communing. I was just a vegetarian standing in a cornfield. What was I missing? Why didn't I think the corn was beautiful, fascinating, a landscape for me to learn like those natural beauties of the West? Why could I think only of feedlots and Frances Moore Lappé and the industrial food system? I worried again that an outsider's judgment could never be overcome, that I wasn't trying hard enough to shake off the preconceived notions of the East Coast to move past seeing Iowa on the surface, a land of corn and plenty, a land of tractors and hogs, a land of industry and growth—with no room for a liberal vegetarian to join in.

OVER THE COURSE of our summer in California, Kevin and I had developed a comfortable rhythm. His job took him out to a remote island fifty miles off the coast for five days at a time, every other week, so we switched off between dedicated time apart, and intense time together. The rotation worked for us, as we each thrived in our separate spaces and appreciated our occasional time together. When I told him in September that I was applying to graduate school, I had no idea whether he would come. For years, we'd done this careful dance, trying to avoid pressuring each other into a life or a decision made only for the relationship's sake, hoping instead that the planets aligned and circumstances fell into place. I hoped he would come, but I didn't want him to feel forced. I couldn't ask, any more than he had ever asked me to come to California.

When I showed him my list of schools, a carefully constructed piece of paper held out tentatively like a blade of grass to test the wind's direction, he took it and made his own version, rewriting the list based on location, in order of the places he'd most prefer to live. Iowa State University was last.

Six months, three acceptances, and one financial aid package later, we moved to Ames, Iowa. Iowa State had been third on my own list, below the schools in locations I knew or wanted to know, but placed relatively high because the master of fine arts program had a special focus on environmental and place-based writing, exactly the kind of work I knew I wanted to do.

When we drove the rented Budget truck into town, getting off Route 30 at the Duff Avenue exit, with its big-box stores and used car dealerships and smoke billowing from the garbage-burning power plant, we sat in silence at the train tracks, waiting behind the lowered gates, as the metal cars covered with yellow and purple graffiti screeched past us along rusted rails, carrying corn oil to the coasts.

I turned to look at Kevin in the passenger seat and said, "I'm so sorry I brought you here."

AS WE SETTLED into our life in Ames, I kept a smile plastered across my face, playing tour guide, pointing out the tiny, fascinating details with immense hope, as if I knew this place somehow, as if I had any idea how to become Midwestern, as if I had thought any more than he had that I would ever end up in the Central Time Zone. I was "Wow, look at all this great produce" at the farmers market, and "Let's ride our bikes to play Scrabble in the park," and "Did you know Ames is right along one of North America's biggest bird migration routes?" I was put-on-a-brave-face. I was bloom-where-you're-planted. He was sullen. He was: "God, it's so flat. God, it's so boring."

I was trying to coax him into happiness, to assuage myself of the guilt of dragging him here. But my happiness and sense of purpose made everything beautiful to me. The trees exploded into flaming color, lining the streets on both sides with bright yellow leaves that stretched over my head and joined hands in the middle of the road. I got a desk in an office and a cadre of instant friends. I was submerged in a life of reading and writing and workshops. My ecstasy with life grew into the town I'd never expected to love, into the leaves and the parks and the birds. I loved everything about Iowa, even when I didn't. I saw potential in the wide, flat land, the soggy black dirt.

When I started my graduate program that August, it became my everything. Whole days, weeks, I camped at my desk on campus, working, plowing straight through a day, often forgetting to eat until dinner. Student papers that needed grading flooded down on me, and I spent all day hunched and scribbling comments, furiously typing my own essays, buried and buried. I thought about the coming winter and wondered what it would look like stretched across this smooth, even Midwestern horizon. When I came home at night, Kevin was already there, hands crusted with soil from the day job he'd found working at the campus botanical gardens. I danced and chattered around him in the kitchen while he washed and chopped vegetables, microwaved our substitute meat products, mixed instant au gratin potatoes. My hands wild with life. His hands cooking for me.

Kevin and I fought a lot in that first year in Iowa—about how much time I spent working and writing, about the close friendships I was developing with the people in my MFA program, about the absence of close friends for him, about sweeping the kitchen floor and washing the dishes. But the gulf was really this: I loved Iowa because I'd found my tribe, and he resented me for taking him away from his. His people were in Montana, and California. My people were here. And I wanted it to be my turn.

When, in winter, an old boss of his called and offered him a job for next summer, we were both a little relieved. This was his dream job, tracking blue- and golden-winged warblers through the forests, catching them in mist nets and holding them in his palms, long fingers curled gently around fluttering wings and fast heartbeats. Inserting syringes, testing their blood. But it was back in New York, just hours from his family. There was a promotion and a pay raise, and of course he had to take it; we both agreed, he had to take it. We would simply spend another summer apart. We had done it before, when I was in D.C. and he was in Montana. We had considered it for California. It was only a few months, and I was so busy. In the end, I think we both knew what was happening, and we both chose to let it happen.

Kevin quit his gardening job in February, though he wouldn't be leaving for New York until April, and took a three-week vacation with his father. He went to Montana, to ride the familiar powder and drink Big Sky beer with his old roommates, his hair winter-long and always flattened beneath a wool hat. I didn't have time to notice he was gone.

Then it was March and the snow started melting, and then it was April and I was waving as his Subaru wagon, packed with a summer's worth of clothes and camping gear and field guides drove towards the interstate, heading east.

In May, I woke up. School was over for the year and I was staying in Iowa, alone. Spring had arrived, fully and with tiny white blooming lilies of the valley in my front yard. Green buds lined the bare branches of winter-worn trees and puckered until bursting. I was triumphant after my first grueling year of graduate school, a prizefighter victorious after twelve rounds, exhausted but burning with joy. I got a haircut for the first time in six months and celebrated the end of the semester by driving north to Minneapolis to see my favorite band play at First Avenue, a downtown club. I spent sixty dollars buying Jameson whiskey for my friends at the Local and stumbled into the concert. When the singer crawled down off the stage into the staggering masses, I pressed drunk into the crowd, felt the heat mingling through sweat-soaked clothes, and wrapped one arm around him while the microphone banged against his teeth. Together, we all screamed and sang. Alone, I made up my mind.

At home in Iowa, I called Kevin and said, "This isn't working."

MY SADNESS WAS colored like Iowa, yellow-brown around the edges, blurring to gold within a few weeks' time. I wept for a few days straight on my bed, then sat up, shrugged, and thought, *I guess you can't have it all.* I was the happiest I'd ever been, but that was never going to be enough to make him happy. Just when I felt like I'd figured out my half of our life, his was crumbling. Our relationship couldn't stand up to my sense of self, my new purpose and independence.

And as I began to articulate myself once again, I needed to ground that identity in place. Whether or not Iowa was the place I'd imagined, I thrust a flag into the black dirt and chose to call it home. If I was alone, I would build my own life. I would give myself over to Iowa, where I'd previously held back for his sake. I would learn to love Iowa. I would learn to feed myself.

I started driving around this new state, whirling in the freedom and slight panic of no one to come home to. When I wondered where Grand Avenue would take me if I kept following it north, I just went north. I learned new curves in new roads and found new towns—not places I would visit, just a general store and a town park and a gas station, but there, like the surprise of a rest stop along an interstate. I finally got around to staining my bedside tables, and to trying that new recipe for teriyaki roasted vegetables. I bought new curtains. I remembered I liked raspberries. Kevin's books were still scattered among mine on the shelves, and I knew the time would come for splitting up silverware, in August, when he would return from New York with a U-Haul to empty my house of his belongings. But the ground around me warmed to my touch, and I felt the beginning of something under my skin.

When I'd moved to Iowa, I was searching for reinvestment. I had been lost, without purpose. Now I had time and no other obligations, and could become fully a part of this new place. Over the three years prior, I'd flitted happily from state to state, trying on different lives, and now I was ready for this one. I wanted to find a community in the place that would be my home for at least another two years. I wanted to work on rebuilding muscle in the spaces I'd let atrophy over the course of our last year of slow descent.

I wanted to move physically, to develop my body and reclaim its health. I ran for the first time in eight months, barely able to make the one-mile loop I'd tried once when we first moved to this house. I started attending yoga class, provided for free at the school's fitness center, four times a week. My yoga mat slung over my shoulder, in flip-flops and capris, I lost myself listening to Radiohead on the bus rides to and from class.

I found myself pleasantly surprised by the Midwest, a certain kind of live-and-let-live social consciousness that, when combined with the state's agricultural past and devotion to a culture of growing, made for a remarkable food scene. Most weeks that summer, I threw my cloth grocery bags into the metal baskets on the back of my bike and pedaled the half mile from my house to Wheatsfield Grocery, the newly expanded version of the local co-op. The walls were painted purple, with murals of smiling animals dancing around cafe tables; the chalkboard sparkled with neon announcements of this week's member specials. Just off to the right of the entrance, the produce section glowed with abundant fruits and vegetables in a light mist. I was ready to begin my new life as a healthy, committed vegetarian. Gone were the days of microwaved pizza snacks and instant mashed potatoes, the overly processed squeeze bags of rice, the canned green beans.

In the ethnic and breakfast food aisle, I gathered a handful of cooking staples. Cascadian Farm cranberry-almond granola for quick breakfasts. Amy's vegetarian refried beans for burritos. Muir Glen organic tomato paste and puree for making my family's pasta sauce. I felt a little guilty picking up any canned goods but convinced myself that buying organic brands from the co-op made a difference. I was used to shopping at massive twenty-four-hour grocery stores that stocked upwards of forty thousand products, all of which came from multinational corporations like Kraft and Heinz and ConAgra, companies that polluted the land and exploited their workers. Buying a cardboard carton of Imagine's organic potato leek soup and depositing it into my cloth grocery bag one aisle over from the grilled tofu sandwiches at the deli *felt* different than buying a can of Campbell's condensed tomato soup at eleven o'clock on a Wednesday night under the fluorescent light of a corporate grocery chain. This was a start.

SOMETIME THAT SUMMER, a friend showed me a chart of organic subsidiary brands of major food corporations.[1] Perhaps whoever created the chart meant it as a guide to help people who would prefer to buy organic to identify the "good" or "safe" brand names at the stores of forty thousand products. But seeing the corporate connections of the organic food industry laid out like that destroyed me. I was in my first step along the path that I thought would help me finally secure the activist eater identity I had always imagined for myself, and I was already facing defeat. One look at that chart and all I could see were the evil corporate overlords pulling the strings behind even my hippie premade food. The granola I bought was from Cascadian Farm, a cooperative originally founded by 1970s back-to-the-landers as the New Cascadian Survival and Reclamation Project. Now, Cascadian Farm is a General Mills subsidiary.

Sure, I reasoned, these large-scale products were still grown organically, without pesticide exposure and with minimal environmental impact, but I soon learned that as the organic industry experienced growth, the pangs of scale and expansion set in. Large corporate food outlets bought up small-scale organic operations that sold because they were struggling to make a profit without a larger market share and shelf exposure. Gerber, Heinz, Dole, ConAgra, PepsiCo—all own organic brands. Horizon's organic cows live out their days on a dry feedlot in the middle of the desert of southern Idaho, eating their organic grain and silage diet shipped in from all points west, being milked three times a day. No antibiotics but still living in a scenario that often makes them sick. Anyone who's ever eaten an

Amy's frozen pizza or burrito can tell you there is such a thing as organic processed food, organic cornstarch, organic snack cakes.

When I saw this corporate organic chart, I couldn't unsee it. Suddenly, the labels in the aisles, even at the locally owned cooperative, changed for me. I saw organic for what it was— one label among many that meant one thing in isolation. I still thought organic was valuable, remembering the threat of methyl bromide in California, the danger to the workers, the frantic washing of consumers. But pesticide-free wasn't *all* I wanted. An organic farm that has a massive manure lagoon or twenty thousand broiler chicken houses was not what I imagined when I recommitted to the co-op. I was looking for something more, some intangible value or principle, some ideal of a more challenging, more ethical food.

When I became a vegetarian, I thought that working harder to get my food would make it automatically more ethical. Vegetarianism, based on what I'd learned years ago in college, was supposed to have a lighter carbon footprint, was supposed to evade corporate conglomerates disobeying federal clean water regulations and disregarding animal suffering. But that summer in Iowa, as I began to question whether anything I'd been attempting to work harder at was worth its own weight, I learned that nothing in the free market is that easy.

I WANTED TO do better, so I kept digging for more information, even as the revelations continued to frustrate me. I began doing my own research into the meat substitute products on which much of my diet relied. According to the Boca Burger website, the birth of this line of veggie burgers happened in Boca Raton, Florida, when a chef decided to construct a veggie burger that actually tasted good. What the website didn't mention was that Boca was "acquired" in 2000 by Kraft Foods, the largest food processing company in North America. And it didn't mention that, until 2007, Kraft was owned by Altria Group—the new and improved name of the public relations–challenged Philip Morris tobacco corporation.

When I started picking away at the corporate connections in the food industry, I began to feel like an Internet crazy, like I'd suddenly become the kind of person who posts on message boards about President Obama's fake U.S. birth certificate, or the government's secret plan to implant microchips in every newborn baby. The more I dug, the more I convinced myself maybe I was just making mountains out of molehills—maybe I was looking too hard for something that wasn't really there. Maybe it didn't have to be so hard. Maybe I could just turn away, go back to my old, easy vegetarian diet.

Until I read that in 2001, a U.S. jury ordered Philip Morris to pay $3 billion in damages to a smoker suffering terminal cancer, a landmark legal victory for the anti-tobacco movement.[2] On appeal later that year, Philip Morris had the punitive damages reduced to $100 million,[3] but even before then, they had raised $9 billion dollars, by selling just 16 percent of Kraft Foods.[4] Suddenly, my purchase of an ethical, meat-free Boca Burger, supposedly free from the stains of corporate greed, just went to helping an evil tobacco corporation avoid sinking into bankruptcy.

Until I also learned that Kraft owns and operates the Oscar Meyer and Louis Rich brands of deli meat and bacon, made from hogs raised and slaughtered by Smithfield Foods, one of the big three pork producers in the U.S., whose manure lagoons flooded most of North Carolina during a late-1990s hurricane, whose felony clean water violations I'd read about when I became a vegetarian. I was buying veggie burgers, but I was right back in the center of the shitstorm.

TWO MONTHS AFTER the end of my relationship, I spent a few hours grading summer school papers in a friend's apartment late one Sunday night. He was teaching out of town for the summer and had left me his key—to bring in his mail, water his plant, and take advantage of his air conditioning and cable TV. My bag waited between the couch and the coffee table as I packed up, lowering the blinds and turning off the air conditioner. But when I took an extra step towards the coffee table, to lean over and shut off the television, my left kneecap brushed up against the corner of the table and slid, with excruciating slowness, out of place.

My foot must have been planted just right, my leg fully extended. I hadn't even hit the table with much force. A single, slight mistake with serious consequences. I toppled onto my back on the couch shouting curses, terrified. In high school, I had dislocated the same knee a handful of times—landed wrong doing a hitch kick at dance rehearsal for a performance of *Joseph and the Amazing Technicolor Dreamcoat*, kneed sideways coming down with a rebound during a basketball game, slid on wet grass playing badminton in my grandparents' backyard—so I wasn't entirely unfamiliar with what had just happened. But those times had been quick, stinging, a sideways click-pop. The pain had been vomit-inducing, radiating through my entire body, but the injury was over as soon as it happened.

This was different. I realized it the moment I landed on the couch and caught a glimpse of my leg. My knee was still out. *My knee was still out.* This gruesome incorrect angle, cocked just to the left of center, geometry so unnatural I felt a wave of hot nausea surge into my chest. *Holy shit.* Panic blanketed me, leaden and lava. A trembling shot through my entire body. I had no idea, *no idea* what to do next. I was stuck in an apartment. I was alone. And I was broken.

After a few quick failed attempts to snap the leg straight myself, to force the joint back into place, I was able to stretch my arm just far enough to get my hands on my cell phone and dial 911. Two hours later, after an IV infusion of morphine and valium, a ride down a flight of stairs on a portable chair carried by two firefighters, a blanket draped over my leg by one who whispered, "You don't need to see that anymore," a shock-induced shiver attack in the back of the ambulance, and an ice pack for the pain at the emergency room, I finally saw a doctor. He took one look at my knee and said, "Yup, that's out. You want me to put it back for you?"

"Yes, please," I replied, forcing a weak smile.

But it was his next question—"Do you wanna not remember it?"—that flooded me with relief. I wept when I realized I could be unconscious for the joint reduction, having seen it happen to my father before, knowing the horrific yank that it would require, the doctor gripping my ankle with his arms and leaning back into it, all his body weight jerking into a single insistent tug. I knew how it looked: my body's resistant bucking, the frantic muscle spasms, the horror-movie screams and seizing.

"Yes," I replied, tears flooding my eyes for the first time all night. I wanted so badly not to remember all that.

They asked me to count backwards from one hundred, and the next thing I knew, I was telling the EMT standing by my shoulder that I was nervous. He looked puzzled, then smiled and told me it was over. It had already happened. I looked down and saw my entire left leg in an immobilizing brace. I didn't remember it—I didn't remember going under or waking up. The last fifteen minutes had been erased from my memory. Less than an hour later, I was on my way out the front door of the hospital on crutches, taking a cab the three blocks back to my own apartment.

THE NEXT MORNING, I woke from a few hours of fitful sleep on my back, a pillow propped under my aching leg. I looked around, disoriented. What would be different now? What would I have to learn to do over again? What would I have to find a new way for? I took a handful of ibuprofen, washed myself in the tub—warned by the doctors not to stand on the weak knee joint without the immobilizer—and headed to school for a few hours of student conferences.

I returned home that evening to make myself dinner, more tired than sore, exhausted from the exertion of hauling myself around on crutches and from a steady diet of painkillers. I hadn't actually experienced much pain the night before. Fear and shock paralyzed me until drugs numbed the physical sensations. Once the leg was reset, while I was blissfully unaware, unconscious, I knew the worst was over. I would start physical therapy in a few weeks to rebuild strength. It felt strange to say it, as I did to my parents on the phone that evening as I reassured them they didn't need to fly out to Iowa to care for me, but dislocating my knee didn't seem like that big of a deal. The whole ordeal, from injury to ER discharge, had taken four hours. I could shrug this off.

For dinner that first night, I cooked myself the simplest thing I could think of, pasta with red sauce: my comfort food.

But when I put the food into a bowl, I realized that, on crutches, I had no way of carrying the food from the kitchen counter to the futon, where I usually ate in front of the television.

I lost it. I burst into tears right there in my kitchen. For the first time since Kevin had left, I realized fully that I was alone. I sobbed, faced with another defeat. My attempts at reformed identity once again fell short, even as I tried to find a new sense of purpose in my writing, even as I tried to eat right, even as I tried to exercise again. I couldn't make it better. And now, in the moment when I most needed something—something so small, just an extra set of hands—I was on my own, with no one to help care for me. I was alone. I was broken. And I couldn't even feed myself.

SUMMER DRIFTED BY in a haze. I turned blame, illogically, outward. Somehow, Iowa had done this to me. I didn't understand why I was failing now, when I had been trying to do better. I had been trying so hard to find a place for myself here. I wasn't going to write off Iowans like I had Montanans. I didn't want my idealism to shroud my vision from the struggles of others, like I had in California. I loved the black dirt, the prairie. I wrote about the native plants and glacial retreats. I wanted to love Iowa. But it had broken me.

I was angry at all of it—how the Iowa air stank of hog shit when the summer winds turned the wrong way. How the cattle penned in at the U.S. Department of Agriculture research facility on my campus had holes in their sides so that researchers could study the havoc a corn diet wreaked on their digestive systems. Suddenly, it felt like Iowa had cost me Kevin, and the security that a partnership brought. Now, there was no one here to help me when I most needed a connection.

I hobbled along, limping and bruised, trying to do better and bumping into things, hitting my head, grazing the sharp corner of reality at every turn. My dislocated knee was a particular challenge in my two-story apartment, where I had to haul myself on crutches up a narrow carpeted staircase every time I had to go to the bathroom. My breathing quickened every time I had to descend the stairs without slipping, without catching a crutch on a stair edge, without leaning too far forward and toppling down. Eventually, I gave up, hopping up the stairs on one foot and sliding down on my butt. Too risky any other way. I spent the day stretched out on my futon downstairs, leg extended, surrounded by protective pillows, taking painkillers, grading papers, watching television, and dozing. I felt nothing short of pathetic.

On my first visit to physical therapy, the therapist measured each of my thighs to compare their muscle mass. This way, she could see how much muscle I'd lost in my left leg since the injury. But she found my left leg to be nearly two centimeters smaller than my right. This was more atrophy, much more, she said, than could have occurred in only two weeks in an immobilizer. I was stunned—despite my efforts towards getting in shape and strengthening my body, my leg had been weaker before the injury.

I felt like I was losing ground, fast. No matter how hard I tried, I couldn't get where I wanted to be. And I was exhausted from trying. I was ready to give up.

When the therapist ended each session with a massage that shifted my kneecap back and forth, I always looked away, nausea souring in the pit of my stomach. It wasn't the weakness of my muscles that sickened me—it was my own fear. I hated how afraid the sight of my own injured leg made me. What I didn't tell the therapist, when she tried to reassure me I'd be back to normal soon, was that I didn't *want* to go back to running or riding my bike. I didn't want to exercise anymore. I didn't want to take any risks. I wanted to ask her if I should just wear a brace for the rest of my life, to avoid tripping down a staircase or stepping off the sidewalk at an awkward angle.

I thought of what the doctor had asked me, the night he reset my leg: "Do you wanna not remember it?"

I did. I wanted to not remember all of this, to forget it had ever happened, and to never let it happen again. I couldn't bear to watch my therapist's kind hands pushing the tiny disc of my patella a millimeter inward, trying to retrain my limp muscles to resist this sideways motion, trying to teach my broken leg to be fixed, because I was too afraid of ever getting hurt like this again.

ONE DAY THAT summer, at the co-op, I waited with a small black brace on my knee, in line behind a guy who, by all outward appearances, looked like an activist vegetarian. He wore the *Adbusters* No Sweat Blackspot canvas sneakers. His Brooklyn hipster facial hair (dark brown and patchy, a messy goatee and moustache) and thick, black-rimmed glasses emerged from a black T-shirt and black skinny jeans. As he unloaded his sparse cart, I noted a bottle of white cranberry juice, a bag of tortilla chips, a jar of salsa, a loaf of bread, and no less than ten containers of Yves brand fake deli ham slices, prepackaged, dull gray.

If I were a different person, if I had still been the girl with the shaved head who stood in the rain at the entrance to my college holding a hand-painted poster that read *No Blood for Oil*, I might have stopped him. I might have shared that I'd eaten my fair share of soy/black bean/mycoprotein meat substitute products, and I might have asked him why he was a vegetarian.

And in that moment, if he had said anything about factory farming, about environmental damage, about corporate ownership or industrial agriculture or fair trade, I might have tried to break him, too. I might have asked him whether he knew that Yves is a product of the Hain Celestial Group, which also owns vegetarian favorites Spectrum organics and Rice Dream nondairy frozen dessert and Tofutown. Whether he knew that Hain Celestial was responsible for the McVeggie, the four-hundredcalorie veggie burger produced by Yves exclusively for McDonald's. Whether he knew that McDonald's serves the McVeggie on a whole wheat bun, slathered in BBQ sauce that, according to signs at the counter, may or may not contain rendered beef fat, signs that also warn the burger may come in contact with meat or chicken during cooking.

I'd have asked him whether he knew that Hain Celestial was a subsidiary brand of the Heinz corporation, one of the top twenty food producers in the world, or whether he could name any other Heinz brands. Smart Ones frozen meals maybe, or Boston Market rotisserie chicken—both of which Heinz makes with chicken bought from Tyson Foods. Tyson, the largest meat producer in the world. Tyson, which in 2003 paid more than $7.5 million in fines for twenty felony violations of the Clean Water Act from manure lagoon pollution seepage and illegal dumping.[5] So, great, you're not eating animal flesh, I might have said. What *are* you eating?

I wanted to ask him the same thing I asked myself that summer: "What good do you actually imagine you're doing?" When buying a Boca Burger means, in no uncertain or abstract terms, helping the defendants in the largest anti-tobacco lawsuit in history avoid bankruptcy. When buying Boca finances additional purchases from Smithfield? What are you avoiding when buying an Yves tofu sausage means helping to establish an exclusive contract with the world's largest and most notoriously unhealthy fast food company? When buying Yves means you might as well be buying from Tyson?

But I didn't ask him any of that. I let him toss his fake meat into his cloth grocery bag and walk out the door, while I bought a box of pasta for myself. It wouldn't have been fair to burden him with my questions. The questions were haunting me because I'd started this, this whole vegetarian, activist journey to make a difference, and I realized it wasn't working. I was beginning to think it was impossible. I didn't ask the poor guy at the co-op to defend himself because I knew once you saw those corporate connections, once you ran headlong into reality, you couldn't unsee them. Just like the gruesome repair of my broken body, I wanted, desperately, to not remember any of this.

But I did.

I didn't ask him because, actually, I was jealous of him. I wanted to return to that naïveté, to the thinking that as long as I wasn't buying meat, I wasn't hurting anybody. As long as I wasn't eating meat, I would be healthy and strong, and my contribution would mean something. I was jealous, because I couldn't believe in that anymore.

Chapter Nine

A Seriously Scrappy Flower

IN LATE AUGUST, as summer began to ignite around its edges into fall, I started having regular dinners with a friend from my MFA program: Scott, who was not a vegetarian. It was Scott's apartment I'd been in when I dislocated my knee, and he joked that his coffee table owed me something, so we sat around it together a few nights a week. These were cook separately, eat together affairs. One night, we walked down the street from his apartment to the co-op for ingredients. I'd already prepared some almond couscous with cranberries for my dinner, and he had some tortillas to use up, so he bought a piece of wild-caught tilapia for fish tacos. I figured since I was at the store, I might as well grab something to round out my meal—a box of frozen Quorn fake breaded chicken cutlets. We got back to his place and took turns with the microwave—me heating my fake chicken, him melting shredded cheddar cheese and salsa spread over his cooked fish—and then sat side by side on the couch, in front of the TV, hunched over our dinner plates.

He actually ate more vegetables than I did that night, if you count the tomatoes, peppers, and onions in his salsa.

Scott and I had bonded during our teacher orientation in our first August in Ames, over a mutual affection for Saddle Creek, the independent music label from his hometown, and we had quickly become close, staying later at the bar than anyone else, commuting to and from campus together. After the end of my relationship with Kevin, we had even more time to spend together. None of our mutual friends were surprised when, by the end of that summer, we started waking up at each other's apartments.

Scott, during our time in Iowa, was a glass-half-empty kind of guy. His short-cropped dark hair and dark eyes drew me in. He was quiet—the kind of person who waited and listened and had everything figured out in his head before he opened his mouth. He joked about everything—even the things he took seriously—and there was no line he wouldn't cross. In this, and in many ways, we were very different. He loved football and basketball and spent most of his autumn weekends on the couch watching sports or playing sports video games on his PlayStation 3. He had a quiet sadness, having lost his father in his early twenties to a painful battle with colon cancer. But we shared a sense of focus in writing. Both of us had come to writing after some time wandering and knew we were in the right place. I was surprised at how hopeful being with him made me feel, how somehow his cynicism was a comfort. How he made me laugh, hysterically, three times a day.

In a new relationship, you want everything shiny and fresh. You want to be the best version of yourself. Frankly, I didn't want my new boyfriend to know that, for the most part, I ate microwaved rice and MorningStar Farms BBQ riblets, so when we ate together, I put my best domestic foot forward. I baked vegetable potpie; roasted potatoes, peppers, and zucchini in a balsamic glaze; and made spinach and tomato quiche. He teased me endlessly about being a vegetarian—as a born and raised Nebraskan, steaks and potatoes and beer were in his blood, but I was determined to convince him that vegetarian food could be good food, too.

As I stretched my imagination to conjure up dinners that would satisfy both Scott's palate and my dietary restrictions, I was forced to notice how many of my vegetarian staples relied on pasta or a box of dehydrated potatoes. In cooking for someone else, I wanted to provide a healthy, balanced, nutritious meal, and this was not at all the kind of meal I had been cooking for myself. I needed to seriously step up my game. In spite of a lifetime of not being much of a cook, the moment I found someone who needed more roughage, there I was in the kitchen, chopping vegetables. Again, I recognized something planted in the long-ago kitchens of my childhood, in the history of spaghetti and meatballs: an incessant desire to nurture with food. I was wary, cautious, suspicious of where that could lead. But I was unstoppable.

I could sense in most of our dinnertimes a sportsmanship—he was game to try whatever vegetarian concoction I placed in front of him, and I was adamant in my defense of the nutritional properties of leafy greens or the heart-healthy perks of bell peppers—but we both knew he really wanted a steak.

ON A WEEKEND trip to we took together to Scott's hometown of Omaha, he took me to his favorite used bookstore, Jackson Street Booksellers in the Old Market, where the owners never say no. There were piles of books stacked precariously in the aisle and against the walls, and we wove our way around the shelves. He snapped cell phone pictures as research for his novel, and I pressed my nose into his upper back. We laughed at the store's indiscriminate taste, finding as much Cormac McCarthy as Dan Brown and Danielle Steele. We kissed noses and softly pinched hips in the back corners of the store, dizzy with new love and old manuscripts. We were brand-new book nerds in love and in our element. We each left with an armful. I finally picked up one book I'd been meaning to read for a while—Michael Pollan's *The Omnivore's Dilemma.*

At the end of that first summer together, we went our separate ways for a few weeks, him to his sister's in California, me back to see my parents in New Hampshire, where I hadn't been for nearly a year. This was summer in the Northeast, a sweaty, thick time, when the pool in my parents' backyard provided a welcome oasis from the heavy morning dew and the black flies. I spent long leisurely hours drinking coffee on the back deck in the mornings with my mother, talking about food.

My mother gave me a tour of her summer vegetable garden. In my memory, the garden had been a small plot of cucumbers and tomatoes, but it now consumed most of the backyard, overflowing with beanstalks and squash blossoms and pea pods. Together, we picked fresh mint, basil, and rosemary from the herb bed, and hung them to dry in the hallways. She showed me the basement shelves lined with crates of homemade salsa and tomato chutney and tomato sauce, the freezer full of fresh corn and green beans and tomato basil soup that would last them through the winter.

I learned that now, my family did, in fact, have a milkman: every Wednesday night, my father put out the empty glass bottles from the week before, to return in exchange for fresh, full ones from their local delivery service. My mother had stopped drinking conventional milk on her doctor's advice after her years-ago hysterectomy because of the bovine growth hormone's estrogen-mimicking properties, but now they had discovered a local source of organic, hormone-free milk.

As I read Michael Pollan, the missing pieces of America's agriculture history came to light: the governmental maneuvers that shifted the global food market and transformed the geographic landscape of the Midwest, my new home, into a single field of corn. Although I'd heard of high fructose corn syrup, I had no idea why it was in everything we ate. Although I knew I'd been eating more processed food than I should be, and had seen those dietary choices add up to more than a couple of extra pounds on the scale, I'd had no idea that maybe there was corn in everything I ate, too, and that all that corn tied me into a system from which I'd thought myself free. I began to trace a line from those crowded cornfields, not to the cattle feedlots I'd been trying to avoid for years but straight into the loaves of whole wheat bread in my own pantry.

With the distance that can only come from adulthood and financial independence, I could finally see my parents as distinct adults, people with their own thoughts and desires and personal investments. My parents' love for food, the love I had thought of as overwhelming and oppressive as a child, still permeated so many of their decisions. But now I could see those decisions as choices we had in common.

Years ago, at my first Christmas as a vegetarian, I ate only side dishes because I insisted my mother go to no extra effort. But in the years that followed, she had, in fact, done so much more for me than I originally noticed or valued. Rather than let her eldest, a vegetarian, sit meals out, she started making pasta sauce in two enormous batches, pouring a third of the giant pot aside in a separate container for me before she added the meatballs. She made two entrees for every dinner I spent in New Hampshire, experimenting with lettuce wraps, vegetable kabobs, couscous-stuffed peppers, anything to make sure I ate more than whatever the rest of my family was eating minus the meat. My father started shopping in the natural foods aisle, stocking the freezer with meat substitutes like MorningStar breakfast sausage patties and Quorn fake chicken breasts for my visits home.

I remembered how, on my first Thanksgiving as a vegetarian, seven years ago, my mother had bought the Moosewood holiday cookbook and dedicated an entire day to crafting a polenta roast. While my father drove to pick me up from college, she spent the day in the kitchen, slowly cooking dry polenta with vegetable broth over a low heat, stirring in dried herbs. She baked the polenta into a wide, flat layer. She made vegetable stuffing from scratch and shaped the cooked polenta around the stuffing: a roulade-style roast. I remembered how, on Thanksgiving Day—after she stuffed the turkey, baked the sweet potatoes, laid out the crescent rolls, all the other dishes—she chopped onions and mushrooms all morning and simmered them into thick vegetable gravy for me. And I remembered that, because I hate mushrooms, she spent half an hour bowed over the sink, straining out every last one.

When I was in college, when I became a vegetarian, food had become more politics than community, more activism than ritual. But now, with time and distance, I began to see that maybe my parents went to all this trouble to keep me close even while I tried to turn away, to maintain our food community in the face of my activism. Maybe they understood that the shared experience of eating together was more important than all of us eating the same thing. Maybe they had radical ideas of their own.

ON THE PLANE ride back to Iowa, as I finished *The Omnivore's Dilemma*, I thought back to a conversation Scott and I had earlier that summer, on the back patio of a bar over a split pitcher of beer, surrounded by colored Christmas lights and smokers. I remembered us talking about our eating habits, our diets, the disappointment we both felt in my attempts at vegetarian cooking. I remember us trying to figure out why we both—educated, privileged, socially conscious—couldn't seem to eat any better.

"I think it's cultural. Look where I'm from," he said, referring to the steaks that made his hometown famous. "If a meal doesn't have meat, even if it fills me up, I still feel as though something is missing."

For so long, I'd assumed the problems with my diet, with my life, were circumstantial: I'd eaten poorly in Montana because vegetarian options were marginalized. I'd eaten better in California because produce was readily available. I blamed my lack of interest in cooking on my desire to be a woman with a career, a woman who didn't have the time to prioritize the kitchen.

Somehow, it hadn't occurred to me that being a bad eater might not be an indictment of my family, or the place I lived, or my politics. It hadn't occurred to me that being a bad eater might just be a symptom of how I thought about food.

I was the problem.

For the first time, I realized this wasn't an issue of me, as a woman, having a dysfunctional relationship with food or cooking. This wasn't a latent feminist feeling resentment towards the kitchen, or an ethical activist being treated as an outsider among hunters. It wasn't nearly so personal.

What I realized was that I was remarkably similar to the stereotypical American eater. I ordered pizzas and drank too much beer. I didn't understand why a person would take the time to simmer white rice and add spices or fresh herbs when they could just buy a plastic bag, squeeze it, and microwave it for ninety seconds. I preferred fast food to handcrafted food, preferred something that came in a box and could be microwaved. For me, those products were made of soy and textured vegetable protein instead of minced white fish or pureed chicken carcass, but this no longer seemed like a meaningful difference. This wasn't about being or not being a vegetarian, or a woman. This was a cultural disorder, plaguing almost all of modern America.

Somehow, in studiously avoiding the connection between food and family, I had neglected to feed myself. When I cooked better because I thought of it as taking care of a man I loved, I was reaching back into my past and resurrecting the notion of food I'd been born into, the sacred ritual of feeding the one you love. Maybe taking care of someone else could become a way to empower, rather than detract from, my own well-being.

Maybe, I thought, there were other complex conversations about food I'd been turning black and white. I thought about migrant workers poisoned by toxic chemicals and severely underpaid while they picked my fresh vegetables. I thought about Adjoa beating cassava root into a safe food for her family, and of all the people who couldn't afford to choose vegetarianism. I thought of the corporate organic brands and saw all the ways in which being a vegetarian meant subscribing to the same agricultural system that produced the factory farms I'd watched in that PETA video. I thought, again, about what good I was really doing.

But rather than again feeling overwhelmed and giving up, I thought about Michael Pollan, and the hope his book had given me. For most of the book, Pollan visits industrial agriculture sites, and sees all the problems I'd been encountering in one way or another for most of my food journey. But later in the book, he visits Joel Salatin's Polyface Farms, and finds a sustainable, biodiverse, inclusive farming operation. When I read Pollan's description of this visit, I could hear his relief on the pages of the book, relief for having found a better way.[1] I understood his frustration, the sense of futility that can come from looking too closely, from wanting to know too much.

I began to wonder whether I might be able to find something else to believe in, too. Maybe I just hadn't been looking in the right places.

AT THE END of the summer, after we returned from our respective trips, Scott moved into a new apartment. With a smaller brace still on my knee, sweating and itchy in the sweltering Midwest sun, I couldn't be much help. When I asked what I could do, he told me to take the plant. Nothing else, he cautioned me, on my still-recovering knee. The plant was an amaryllis that I'd been watering for him all summer.

I've never been good with plants. I always forget to water them—even when they're right in front of me—or I put them out into the elements too early in the season, or some freak accident occurs—bunnies nibbling my otherwise healthy basil. The day after I dislocated my knee in his apartment, I went back up that flight of stairs on crutches to water the amaryllis. I was working against twenty-six years of killing plants, and this one belonged to someone I really wanted to impress. Somehow, I kept the amaryllis alive for two months on my own.

On moving day, I put the amaryllis on the floor in the front seat of my car for a trip to his new place, and then stayed behind while he drove the moving truck over. I sat in the empty stairwell, by an open door, reading and stretching my sore joints and waiting for the carpet cleaners. Unfortunately, the plant didn't fare so well in the car, with all the windows up, in the direct sunlight, for two hours. When I met him at the new apartment, I emerged sheepishly from my car and said, "I think I killed your plant."

Those big, beautiful green stems, tall as hope, had wilted, turned dark olive green like leaves just before autumn. They had collapsed on themselves and started to shrivel. When I lifted it up out of my car and showed the drooping amaryllis to him in his new apartment, he just laughed. This wasn't some massive domestic failure, not any kind of judgment on me as a girlfriend or person. We joked that I'd done so well, but it couldn't be helped—my black thumb was a lifelong curse. Two hours in my care had maimed the amaryllis.

The next morning, before he left for his last week in Omaha, Scott gave me the extra set of keys to his apartment. Mine for good. And kissed he me on the forehead and told me it was my responsibility to rehabilitate the amaryllis. I decided I was going to kick ass at plant nurturing.

I'd reawakened that summer, because I remembered that being an activist isn't just about refusing to do something. Activism is a belief in action—in the inherent value of digging your hands in, messing around, and building something new. A belief in voting and caretaking and laying deep roots. Growing the amaryllis was no longer about being a good girlfriend.

It was about cultivation. I was going to do this right. I opened my laptop to research the care and needs of an amaryllis—and I discovered it wasn't an amaryllis at all.

The real amaryllis is a delicate thing, a native of South Africa, also called the naked lady. It typically blooms indoors, in the winter, tissue-paper pink and white petals unfolding gracefully, a ballerina flower. But what Scott had was a bright, flashy thing—a hippeastrum, whose unremarkable stems are often mistaken for amaryllis stems. The hippeastrum is a whole different beast: a big, red, showy flower, loudly announcing itself to the world, fire engine in the snowy winter. Although the bulb is tender and should not be exposed to frost, the flower grows quickly and with ease. Its name means horseman's star, and it is believed to be named after a medieval weapon. A seriously scrappy flower.

I got it a new pot—not a cheap, disposable plastic thing— and set the plant in the soil of its solid pottery home. I reburied the bulb deeper in the wet, black dirt, so that the plant would be better prepared to hold up its own burgeoning weight. I trimmed back those wilted tips of green stem to a more reasonable height, undoing months of growth, a gesture of faith. I let myself into Scott's new apartment. And I put the morning star on the coffee table that dislocated my knee, by the window, to greet him new and alive when he got back.

WHEN I WENT to the Ames farmers market for the first time that September, I had a purpose. I was on a mission. Bolstered by Michael Pollan, by Scott, by the memory of my family and their way of thinking about food, by the ethics that had guided my initial decision to become a vegetarian, I took charge. I went to find my better way. I wanted to find a source—just one farm, one market, one something—that I could trust: someplace that I could just believe in.

The remains of the last young fruits of summer waited in small bunches along the checkered cloth–lined stalls, gathered in bright colors in their wooden crates. As I made my way around the old train depot that held the market, selecting little baggies of snow peas and green beans, handling tomatoes in purples and oranges, squeezing ears of corn and curvy bell peppers, something weird happened. People started talking to me.

I bought a cucumber from Paula of Twin Girls Garden from Madrid, Iowa, and when I commented that the name of her farm was adorable, she nodded in the direction of the giggling blonde girls sitting under the white tent with her. Her face breaking into a smile as she turned back towards me, she explained that she named the farm after her daughters, her inspiration. For Paula, raising her girls healthy meant plenty of sunshine, fresh air, and fresh produce, so she ramped up her hobby garden into a full-fledged farm, using only natural, chemical-free pesticides and fertilizers. A couple of years ago, she saw how the farm could become self-sustaining by producing its own fertilizer, so the girls added a couple of sows to the mix and started selling pork products. As I left with my cucumber, Paula told me she kept a farm stand open all week in the summers—a table and a cash box on the side of her long dirt driveway, an honor system, where people take what they like and leave the money. She told me to swing by, anytime.

I bought a gallon of nonhomogenized, or cream top, milk from Picket Fence Creamery, where daughter Jenna and father Jeff manned the booth. I'd had this milk before, purchased from Wheatsfield Co-op, and I knew that nonhomogenized fat content made for a thicker, more flavorful milk. As I waited for my change, I fingered a brochure they had on the table about Sample Sundays. Jenna explained that once every couple of months, they invited people out for a free-for-all at the farm, to tour the grounds and see the cows grazing on fresh pasture, to raise awareness of the store they have on-site, where they also sell meat and dairy from ninety other farms. They roll out the big grill, sell brats and burgers, host a local live band, and let people wander, sampling cheese curds and ice cream.

Jenna told me they just wanted people to feel comfortable visiting the farm. They kept it open to the public year round but found if they set a day and time, the party was pretty popular and put their customers at ease about where their dairy came from. I bought the milk and used my change for a half gallon of chocolate ice cream, which is still the best, silkiest, most melt-in-your-mouth chocolate I've ever tasted, not overly rich but still soft with sugar.

I wandered into the indoor section of the market and picked a dozen eggs out of the cooler. When I paid at the register, the woman who rang me up smiled at the label on the carton.

"You've got to go say hi to Cindy," she said, gesturing towards the name of the farm. "She's outside with the honey and her weekly cooler." She pointed out the table to me before going back to her knitting.

I walked over to Cindy, waving, shook her hand, and said, "I just wanted to say thanks for the eggs. What else you got out here?"

Cindy showed me the honey and beeswax candles she made, and then flipped open the white cooler at her feet to reveal frozen, shrink-wrapped, bloody packages of meat. She began listing them off: "Brats. Pork chops. Tenderloin. Whole roasters. What're you looking for?"

A bit startled, I instinctively said, "Nothing, thanks." But I was curious and stayed to talk more about the farm. Both Cindy and her husband, Vic, like many of my students, came from generations of farm family but realized when they had children there was something broken in the way they practiced agriculture. A farm, Cindy said, shouldn't be a place too dangerous for children. She was tired of telling the boys to stay off the massive machinery or to stay inside on days their parents sprayed the fields with pesticides.

She and Vic decided to reclaim the farm, to return to what their agricultural heritage had once been. First, they began a new rotation. They abandoned the traditional corn/soy planting schedule and started growing and harvesting non-genetically modified corn, soy, barley, and hay, using natural nutrient cycling by feeding those crops to their animals and composting the animals' waste to fertilize the plants. The livestock were raised without hormones, drugs, or meat by-products, because, as Cindy said, if you keep the hogs in a clean place, they'll stay that way.

Cindy said the part about her new farm she'd found most rewarding, the part that made it all feasible, was being able to welcome customers directly in. People loved to look at the photos of happy hens and hogs roaming on the farm. It was the ideal they were all hoping for, and when they saw the farm, it became real. When they asked for details, she could provide them. When people toured the Madsen farm, sometimes their toddlers screamed and cried at the sight of baby chicks—the little batty creatures so unfamiliar to suburban children—but no one ever left disappointed. When people had the opportunity to ask questions, they formed a deep trusting bond with the farmers who were finally willing—and able—to be open and honest. It was what kept people coming back, Cindy said, and what kept them motivated to do all the extra work.

I left Cindy, and the farmers market, that day, with a lot of answers to the practical, literal questions I'd had about standards and practices and pesticides, about organic certification and genetic modification. But I had a whole slew of new questions.

Throughout the summer, I had begun to see that the idea of eating ethically was significantly more complex than I'd originally thought. I'd constructed a world in which food was a black-or-white issue, a series of dichotomies with a rigid line down the middle. Conventional versus organic, industrial versus sustainable. But on which side of the aisle should I place the industrial organics, like Kraft-owned Kashi, or Oscar Meyer–owned Boca? And where should I put someone like Cindy?

Until then, my most serious distinction about food was the one between meat eater and vegetarian. I hadn't changed my mind at all about Tyson or Smithfield or Cargill. But all along, I had been trying to take action. Maybe, instead of opting out, I could find a way in. I could insert myself into a positive, beneficial food community. I could participate. At the Ames market, I had discovered a way to make the difference I had wanted to make when I became a vegetarian. Could I—should I, as an ethical eater—consider buying a chicken from someone like Cindy Madsen? I'd been looking for something to believe in, and I thought I'd found it. But it didn't look anything at all like I'd expected.

Sometimes, I decided, you have to give up your expectations. Sometimes you have to lose it all. Sometimes you have to take the risk of casting off the love you had for five years to find the one that fits you better. Sometimes you have to suffer great injury to understand how much pain you can handle. I only saved the amaryllis after I killed it. I only saw the possibility in Cindy Madsen's chicken once I acknowledged full on the flaws in my old ways of thinking about food. I had to lose hope in my brand of vegetarianism in order to take the action that was going to do the good I truly believed in. And so, in early September, I bought my first chicken in seven years.

Chapter Ten

Tastes Like Chicken

THE TEXTURE WAS the strangest thing. After nearly seven years—five skipped Thanksgiving turkeys; six passed-over prime rib Christmas dinners; one very depressing trip to the Charlie Palmer steakhouse in Washington, D.C.; and one thoroughly unpleasant digestive experience after the bowl of *pepe* soup laced with traces of goat meat in Ghana—after all the internal and external debate, my first mouthful of chicken and all I could think was: *I'd forgotten how hard you have to work to chew this stuff.*

For the better part of three hours before the meal, and for the month it took between my meeting Cindy Madsen and buying my first chicken, I had been mentally and physically preparing to eat meat again. First, I discovered that Cindy only sold whole chickens, and I wasn't quite prepared to disassemble a solid frozen mass. Yet. Since this would be my first chicken in so long, I decided not to go completely outside my comfort zone, and instead of buying directly from Cindy, I bought a package of skinned and boneless breasts from Wheatsfield Co-op. I'd researched Wheatsfield's source: Ferndale Market, a Midwestern cooperative of family-owned, organic, and sustainable meat producers. I might not have been buying directly from a farmer, but I was inching closer to what felt right.

I stood alone in the kitchen, slowly stirring pasta sauce with the big wooden spoon that my mother taught me was the staple kitchen utensil. I had made, as usual, far too much sauce for two people, because I only knew the ratios in large batches. The sharp scents of garlic, basil, black pepper, and Parmesan tingled inside my nostrils, floating up from a big copper-bottomed saucepan, simmering over a low heat. Fresh snapped green beans waited in a second saucepan for the burner to click beneath them. The shrink-wrapped breast of a chicken that had very recently pecked grubs from cow manure, a chicken that had bobbed its white, feathered head to the dirt of a nearby farm, sat defrosting on a Fiestaware plate on the counter.

The details were important, carefully culled to construct this meal. Green beans for the fiber, to help with digesting my first bites of meat in nearly seven years. Ziti with Nona's pasta sauce for comfort, familiarity. Scott was the chicken cook, because I'd never actually cooked meat before. The chicken breast from a family-owned integrative poultry farm, chicken raised on pasture with a diet containing no hormones, no antibiotics, and no animal by-products. Farmers who partnered with a locally owned slaughterhouse to process the chicken in a minimal, clean, humane way.

Processing the animal means killing it. Slaughtering it dead, then dismantling the body and repackaging it into the pieces we Americans can stand to look at, and will eat. Although the term had always sounded to me too clinical, too euphemistic, creating a distance between the customer and the death, I was beginning to hear a different meaning there.

I wanted to get better, too. All these details I chose as part of my process, to redefine the boundaries between human as eater and animal as food, to forge a new relationship, to begin to taste the fertile agricultural lands of the Midwest that were now my home.

New Age organo-hippie as it sounds, I wanted to honor the chicken. I wanted this time to be different.

SCOTT AND I entered into the preparation of the chicken together. We planned the menu. He suggested cutting it up and mixing it in with something my body considered normal, to stave off potential digestive disruption. I decided on pasta, the sacred ritual of the Italian, easily my most commonly eaten meal but also the one I turned to when I needed a reminder of a mother, a family wrapping their arms around and nurturing me.

On the big night, Scott opened a bottle of 2001 reserve Chianti from Tuscany to toast the special occasion. I set the table—fork and knife, paper towel napkin. He laid out the safety regulations for me in the kitchen: Don't use the same utensil or plate for both the cooked and uncooked meat. Since we were at Scott's apartment, we cooked the chicken his way: the admittedly impersonal George Foreman grill, whose handbook says six minutes for a chicken breast, but Scott did seven just to be safe. Check the insides. See any pink? Cook for another minute. He explained the steps of cooking as he went, how he usually seasoned the chicken. We chose oregano to echo the tomato sauce, rosemary to complement the white meat.

When the grill was ready, I watched over his shoulder as he sliced open the plastic, peeled it backwards off the slimy pink breast, and sprinkled the herbs across the chicken. *This is the first step,* I thought, *we are transforming animal to food.* When he slid the tines of the fork into the chicken and lifted it from its package, I caught sight of the bloodline on the underside of the breast and startled a bit. This now-cold slab of meat once had veins and muscle and a heartbeat. This creature that once lived had died so that I could eat it. I made sure to look straight at the chicken when he set it against the black ridges of the grill and closed the cover. Seven minutes until dinner.

I STOOD AWKWARDLY in the kitchen while we waited for the chicken to cook, feeling more removed from the meat than I expected to, shifting my weight back and forth between nervous feet, stirring the pasta, testing the tomato sauce, sliding my fork into the beans, repeating. The grill hissed and sputtered on the counter. Tendrils of smoke snaked up from the sides, and I leaned in to smell them, picking up only the vaguest scent of oregano, tinged with something unfamiliar. Something smoky, like a campfire or popcorn burning in the microwave. Right. Flesh. This was flesh. Thinking of the chicken this way gave me pause, my stomach spinning slightly. What if it made me sick? What if I didn't even like the taste of meat anymore?

The doubts of the summer came rushing back, my finely honed guilt reflex kicking up in the back of my throat. Was this a pointless exercise? Was I simply justifying a desire to eat meat again with the theory that I'd do more good supporting local, sustainable, humane farming? Was there such a thing as ethical meat eating? The worries still moving around under my skin stemmed from the fact that I was still struggling to define what any of those words meant—and what they meant to me.

I'd seen enough to make me wonder about any company's accurate use of the concepts of local food, sustainable growth, ethical agriculture. I'd seen Monsanto commercials extolling the eco-friendly virtues of Roundup Ready soybeans genetically modified to be resistant to the eponymous herbicide, describing the corporation's devotion to the Iowa soil they poisoned. I'd seen how illogical a local foods label could become when you lived within ninety miles of a Tyson packing plant. I'd seen organic avocados flown in from Argentina, and I'd been told that high fructose corn syrup was good for my body.

I was beginning to worry that this was a pointless endeavor—that no matter how hard I tried, I would find it impossible to identify everything I ate, to trace each ingredient back to its source and be ethically satisfied. I could see myself giving up after a few weeks, frustrated and disillusioned, unable to believe there was such a thing as sustainable agriculture, as humanely raised meat.

But I was so tired of being disillusioned. And I had begun to feel that my disillusionment was a choice. My goal in becoming a vegetarian had been to abandon the current food system, to stay out of it altogether, to go back in time, to before these crimes against animals and the land had been committed. But that time wasn't real—or it certainly never had been for me. I never lived in pioneer times. My suburban family had never grown all our own food or sewn all our own clothes. When those times had existed in our country's past, I could imagine the pioneers themselves willingly and eagerly abandoning them, putting away their horse-drawn plows for tractors and happily trading in a fleet of backyard chickens for the grocery store.

A great, new distance exists between the back-to-the-land ideal and the supermarket textured vegetable protein burger owned by a bacon-curing corporation. All I could do now was navigate my way through the space between. I could, and would, drive towards my ideal, but I would try to remember that perfect, harmless food didn't exist, and didn't have to. I wanted to believe in my food, to remember where it came from and what it took to raise it, to be honest about what that growth process took and who died along the way, rather than pretend these deaths didn't exist in lieu of the pioneer ideal. I was reentering meat eating to reclaim food as a responsibility, to myself, my body, my health—to the land. To remember the source of food. To believe again by looking closely and knowing exactly what was there, messy and complicated as the picture may be.

Maybe there would never be one perfect farm. Maybe I could find hope in letting go of the idea that there had to be.

AND SO I sat down with my chicken. With my plate in front of me, I took a sip of wine and a deep breath. I got both pasta and chicken in the first bite, just to be safe. I chewed, slowly. Swallowed. No vomiting yet. Took another bit and, this time, thought about it, let the cube of chicken roll around on my tongue, testing it between my teeth, allowing myself to taste it, to think of the rosemary.

I have never been so conscious of a meal in my life—which was kind of the point. The meat was chewy, a little tough; it stuck my jaw together, making the muscles work harder. Juices leaked from the chicken and pooled in the corner of my mouth. I sucked on the chicken again, to draw out more of the sweet flavor.

I thought of my vegetarian classmate, on the day I decided to become a vegetarian, saying we had to face it, had to look at the animals' death in order to earn our right to eat them. I thought about all the other things I'd learned—about migrant workers' labor conditions and corporate organic brands' environmental practices—all the other things I wanted to be sure I looked at, carefully.

I knew this meal was only the first step. I still had questions, and I still had to figure out a way to marry my desire to be more fully invested with my fears of disappointment, of what I might find.

I wondered how to describe the taste—so specific—and could come up with only one word: chicken. It simply tasted like chicken, a moist, savory, chewy thing I would have to learn all over again. And then, with the chicken still in my mouth, as my teeth worked the meat up and down, I forced myself to think of a living chicken, to think of it as an animal, to picture the yellow feet pulling apart grasses, to picture small piles of smooth, speckled eggs.

To my surprise, I didn't gag, or spit out the chicken. I felt a surge of emotion somewhere behind my chest and smiled, thinking of this creature that had lived on grass, that had lived as a chicken, that had died. I felt a sort of grateful fondness, and I swallowed.

"Well?" Scott asked, turning to face me. "What do you think?"

I nodded, and smiled, then took another bite. "Tastes like chicken."

Chapter Eleven

How to Dissect
a Chicken

WHEN I LOOKED closely, it quickly became clear that the bloody, yellow-skinned lump of frozen-rock-hard chicken was a long way from shredded chicken quesa-dillas for dinner that night. I spent a few long minutes turning the block in my hands over the sink, looking through the skin and plastic for some familiarity, some recognition of this as either food or animal. This time, I'd bought my chicken directly from Cindy Madsen. Turns out, when you placed an order for a chicken directly from a farmer and checked the box labeled "cut up" instead of the one labeled "whole" that didn't mean you got the pieces trimmed and cleaned and packaged in shrink-wrap and Styrofoam the way they come at the grocery store.

In my defense, I was a beginner here. This was just two weeks after my chicken with pasta, after a seven-year hiatus during which I finished college, got my first apartment, and started learning to cook for myself in earnest. I barely knew how to cook at all, and my knowledge was limited to the meatless meal. Before this week, my experience cooking and preparing meat had been restricted to setting the dinner table while my mother sautéed in the background. I had no idea what a chicken looked like in the stages between being a live chicken and being breaded chicken tenders with a side of fries. But I did want to learn. I knew if I was going to be a meat eater again, I had to remember what had made me stop eating it in the first place; I couldn't succumb to the convenience and remove of the grocery store. I needed to know what a dead chicken looked like.

That night, I turned to one of my more reliable sources of information on all things random: HowStuffWorks.com. A quick search for "how to cut up chicken" revealed just the article I needed, complete with step-by-step directions and images to lead the way. I left the chicken out overnight to defrost. The next afternoon, I pulled out the cutting board, emptied the sink of dirty dishes, got out a few plastic bags for debris, and set to work learning how to dismantle a chicken.

THE FIRST THING I had to do was figure out what I was working with. The How Stuff Works article had directions for cutting a whole chicken into halves and quarters, into pieces, into Chinese-style chicken, for skinning, deboning, slicing, and dicing. I used a knife to open the shrink-wrapped plastic bag and dug my hands right into the body of the chicken, gently pulling on the outer edges to see where it would come apart. The legs and wings folded outward, creaking with the slow crack of half-melted ice, but the breast stayed intact, and I could see the ridges of the spine running along the length of the chicken. I pushed around the instructions with my elbows, palms already olive-oil greasy with raw meat, and studied the black-and-white images as if trying to discern a route by staring at the squiggly red lines on a map, looking for something like the chicken in front of me. Best I could tell, before freezing it, someone had cut this chicken into an undivided breast, whole legs, and wings, and then folded them all back together like some macabre autopsy survivor. I would have to separate the breast, separate the legs into thighs and drumsticks, remove the back and breast bones, and skin the whole thing.

I'd spent seven years as a vegetarian because I never wanted to have to look at a chicken this closely. For most of my life, I'd studiously looked away from the animals I was eating, wanting badly to forget the big milk-eyed cows at the state fair while I enjoyed my New York strip and horrified by the occasional vein I could spot beneath the lemon herb breading on my haddock filet. I hated eating lobster—blasphemy in coastal New England—because it looked too much like the animal it had once been. I preferred breaded, fried chicken tenders to wings or drumsticks, canned tuna to tuna steaks, preferred not to think about the living thing while I ate its dead body. But if I was really going to do this—eat meat in order to become a more integral and intentional part of my food system and my community—I needed to face my initial source of disgust. However much it disturbed me, I could no longer look away from the facts of body and blood and bone that went into eating animals.

Locate the joint by moving the thigh back and forth with one hand while holding the drumstick.

I stood in the kitchen with the chicken, prepared to interact for the first time with my food as a dead animal, ready to confront the anatomical reality that went into making my meal. And it really grossed me out. I grabbed the chicken's leg with both hands and slowly worked the joint as the directions suggested, surprised at how smoothly and easily it moved. The leg of a chicken bends in the opposite direction from that of a human, and as I gently pushed up on the bottom knob of the drumstick, the thick meaty thigh moved in response. I could see this working as a joint. I could imagine the leg, covered in fine white feathers, lifting a grotesque yellow talon into the air in the jerking, careful walk of live chickens.

I wasn't sure what to make of the object in my hand. In some ways, it appeared so animal, in some ways a leg, the buttery skin pocked with follicles like pores, dotted the way my own skin is in places. But detached from its body, scalded clean of feathers, cold and animated only by me—a chilling marionette—the leg reminded me of nothing so much as it did food. I didn't really recognize it as part of a once-living creature, but I did recognize the Z-shaped wings from those I'd seen slathered in thick orange buffalo sauce at sports bars. I could clearly see the bulges of meat lining the bones of the drumstick, pulled taut to the edges. My goal was deconstruction, to convert this leg into those parts, so I laid the leg down on the plastic cutting board and went to work.

Place the leg, skin side down, on a cutting board. Cut completely through the joint. Repeat with the other leg.

Not really sure where I was supposed to cut, incredulous that this would even work, I just started cutting somewhere near the middle of the leg, trying to clear the skin out of the way so that I could identify the center. The knife—just a standard chef's knife I'd acquired at Target at some point in my twenties, and whose blade had mostly sliced bell peppers until now—slipped a bit against the flesh, piercing the skin but not slicing the meat, just pushing it around. I switched to a serrated blade, one of the steak knives from my block, and dug in with more force—and felt the muscle give, catch against the grated edge of the knife, and tear. I realized I had no idea what kind of knife I was supposed to be using, if I had the right knives, or if they were sharp enough, after years of vegetarian use, for this job. Eventually, I could see the bright white ball of the joint fitting into its socket. I stopped cutting and lifted the leg again, watched the joint function as a perfect anatomical specimen while I moved the drumstick and thigh back and forth.

I'd seen bone before, human and animal, but the intricate inner workings of our bodies always left me shaking my head in slight disbelief. I thought back to the X-rays I'd recently seen of my own dislocated knee and recalled that human knees don't work like chicken knees. Human knees aren't ball and socket joints—but our hips are. This gave me pause. Considering the joint of the chicken's leg I was about to break similar in any way to a part of my own body made me cringe. I needed to dislocate this joint, and the memory of that pain still lingered fresh in my own body. Although the animal was long dead and past suffering, I knew I was about to injure the chicken, to render its body broken.

I readjusted my grip on the slippery yellow skin and tried to yank the two pieces of the leg apart, producing slight cracks and one convincing pop but not breaking anything. I bent the joint in the wrong direction. Still no success. Back to the knife. I thought about wedging the tip of the blade in between the ball and socket and prying but, fearing for the safety of my eyes, decided just to cut through the bone. This was surprisingly easy. Not exactly what the instruction suggested but not the first time I'd deviated from a recipe. I took the blade to the bone with quite a bit of force, imagining I was holding a hack-saw and performing an amputation. But the serrated blade only needed a couple of quick, insistent slices, scarring the bone enough that I could break it. No shards splintered out, just a clean snap.

Now I was in uncharted territory—bone marrow. I could see the complex underworld of a chicken bone, the spongy pink mesh that lived inside the skeleton, still laden with red blood cells.

I gagged and dropped the broken leg to the counter, leaning into the sink in case I vomited. As I hung my head, eyes closed, nose plugged to block out the dank scent welling up from the carcass, I wondered again why the hell I was doing this. What kind of person wants to see these things? Wouldn't it just have been easier to stay a vegetarian and never have to know what chicken bone marrow looked like? Why was I even bothering? I felt so sick, my stomach churning with hyped-up acid, that I wondered whether I'd ever be able to actually eat this particu-lar chicken.

But this was a journey of self-actualization and I was deter-mined not to walk away or give up. I understand the world by feeling it. To experience a true connection to my food, to really understand the sacrifice at stake in eating meat, I had to dig in with my bare hands. I had to let go of my salmonella fears, my squirmy discomfort with flesh. I needed to look. This is how I found myself, eyes watering, shining-wet knife in hand, mouth-breathing to avoid the gradually building sour smell, snapping ribs and sawing the heart-shaped breast of the chicken away from its backbone.

Cut through any remaining connective tissue and pull the breast away from the backbone. Slip the point of the knife under the long rib bone on one side of the breast. Cut and scrape the meat from the rib bones, pulling the bones away from the meat.

Now, I began to feel vaguely hunter-gatherer. No matter that I was using a knife from Target—there was something undeniably primal about sawing through flesh, about the grating feeling that shivered up my arm each time the blade slipped and made sideways contact with the rib bones. I was scraping meat away from skeleton. Taking a kill—albeit not my own—and harvesting it. I was pulling the carcass out from the inside.

The flesh of the breast peeled back from the bone easily, and the serrated blade moved through the soft tissue without a struggle, just a few pink shreds left hanging on to the backbone. I laid the thick piece of smooth flesh onto the cutting board. I examined the fine white tendons like the roots of a tiny plant reaching into the soil, the traces of a bloodline where the backbone had once been. Then I realized what I was left with, what I was still holding: a ribcage, complete with dangling chicken heart. I put the knife down.

Given the size and amount of meat splayed on the cutting board, the smallness of the ribcage mystified me. I could hold it, cradled in both my hands, and did, hovering over the sink for a few long minutes, running my thumbs lightly along the delicate curved rib bones. Blood smeared against my left thumb and I stared at it, stared at the evidence of life and death I held right there in my palm. I stared at the blood because I was trying not to stare at the heart.

I wanted so badly to touch the heart, but somehow it felt mildly inappropriate, a sort of invasion, for a human finger to ever come in direct contact with that most crucial organ of any other life-form. But then I remembered that people get autopsied and hunters fish bullets out of deer hearts and some people even eat chicken hearts and the other pieces bundled neatly into that plastic bag labeled "giblets." I was sawing this chicken apart, and so I touched it. I touched just one hesitant index finger to the dangling heart, a shriveled cranberry in an open-air cage, then jerked my hand back quickly.

In an opinion piece for the *New York Times*, Roger Cohen suggests that Americans tend to prefer excised chicken breasts, plastic packaging, and gloved hands to my current visceral, bloody approach to food, because we are, in fact, terrified of the innards of the animals we eat. The guts, he says, reek of life.[1] Maybe all we're scared of is being reminded of just how much we resemble an animal on the inside, too. I'd never seen a real heart—of any animal—before. This was unbelievably, impossibly tiny, no bigger than my thumbnail. I was in awe. I just stood and stared for quite a while, then carefully laid the entire ribcage in the sink. I watched as gravity tipped the heart backwards until it rested against the backbone, and left the carcass there while I, newly serious, went back to the business of converting life into food.

Place the breast, skin side up, on a cutting board. Split the breast into halves by cutting along one side of the breastbone.

Now I had wings, thighs, drumsticks, and breasts: food. Months ago, when I started the process of investing more deeply in my food, I thought that if anyone faced up to the fact that their steak was a cow and their bacon was a pig, they would surely look away in disgust. I'd spent most of my life sure that thinking of food as an animal would necessarily preclude you from being able to eat that animal, especially if you could visualize its life and inevitable death. But after I touched that heart and laid it down, I felt a strange and distant respect for the animal that was entirely separate from thinking of it as food. I still didn't think I'd be able to eat chicken for dinner that night. But I was no longer gagging.

With fingers, work along both sides of the breastbone to loosen the triangular keel bone; pull out the bone.

I pressed my fingers against the flesh of the chicken, like pulling a lost drawstring back towards the opening, and a small pointed white bone emerged from the tip of the breast. After a few slippery losses, I slid the bone up and out of the inside of the chicken breast.

Cut the meat away from the wishbone with the tip of the knife. Grasp the tip of the wishbone and slowly pull it out of the breast, making sure not to snap it.

Once I'd freed the edges of the wishbone, carefully, with just the sharp point of the blade, I used my thumb and fore-finger to grasp the very top, the little point that some neutral party is supposed to hold after Thanksgiving dinner, and slid it, slowly, up out of the breast. When the dishes were scraped clean, as the last few uncles mopped up gravy with crescent rolls, and grandmothers stacked bones and remnants of skin on one plate to carry over to the trash, this was the part of the turkey that was left, this was the part that you wished on. I stood over the sink in my kitchen, still breathing more shallowly than usual. I was pretty sure it'd be bad luck to snap the wishbone on the first chicken I'd ever dissected. Still, I wondered whether I could snap it by myself, or what I would even bother to wish for.

I decided I was pretty lucky. Instead of a wish, I could only think of blessings, of thanks. This was an endeavor already so laden, in my own mind, with meaning and potential, that wishing on or cracking the bone seemed trite. Hokey. Unnecessary. Plus, maybe in bad form, for the chicken's sake. So I laid the wishbone, intact, beside the snapped ribcage in the plastic bag in the sink.

Grasp the skin with a clean cotton kitchen towel to improve your grip. Take the towel and pull the skin away from the meat.

Just the word skinning made me uncomfortable, possibly because of its association with childhood injuries, a frequent occurrence for me, usually targeting the knees. I pictured bloody scrapes, pocked with fragments of loose pavement embedded under the skin as they scabbed over. I pictured creepy guys in red flannel shirts practicing taxidermy, or converting downed grizzlies into bearskin rugs. For some reason, this step of making my chicken edible seemed more grotesque than any other, as if stripping the chicken of its skin was more invasive than snapping its backbone or touching its heart. I felt like removing the skin was my final act of defiance against the chicken, my insistence on making it palatable for human consumption. But I bought skinless chicken breasts at the grocery store, believing the absence of the fatty skin made the meat healthier, and I was determined to really know what went into making them look the way I saw them in the freezer section.

Skinning was hard work. Since I was nearing the end of an hour with the chicken, I was growing impatient, still interested in finishing the job but eager to get back to the papers that needed grading, the plants that needed watering, the television that needed watching. Skinning was seriously slowing me down. I used paper towel to improve my grip, not sure if any of my brightly colored kitchen towels were clean enough to use on raw chicken. This was absolutely necessary, despite the suggestive tone of the direction. When I tried to peel the skin backwards off the thigh with a paper towel—well, that's how I lost one thigh to the dirty kitchen floor.

Starting was easy. Make a small slit in one end of the skin and pull. The yellow skin, white on the inside, folded backwards over itself without much difficulty. But there came a point of critical mass, somewhere around the middle of a thigh, or near the bulge of a drumstick, at which the skin became backed up against itself, providing too much friction for even the paper-toweled hand to go much farther.

The white inner fascia stuck to the pink flesh, as if sewn on some internal seam. As I pulled, hard, on the flaps of squishy, fatty skin in my right hand, I could hear the muscle of the chicken giving, this slight sucking noise, an impossible suction. I twisted my wrist, doubling the stretched-out, flopping skin over the back of my hand, and yanked harder but still couldn't part the chicken from its skin. I took the knife out again and laid the drumstick sideways on the cutting board, pressing a paper towel down on the skin and sawing through it, leaving small shreds of skin still stuck, dangling, on the tip of the drumstick. Good enough. One down—one drumstick, one thigh—two breasts to go.

I stood bent over the kitchen counter, grunting slightly, yanking at a half-exposed drumstick, trying to roll the wet skin over itself bit by bit, and it was somewhere in all this that I realized I was no longer dealing with an animal. The work was hard, messy, and completely undignified. This was no longer a ceremonial approach to honoring the life of the chicken by recognizing it as a living thing. There was no element of prayer or ritual. I was pulling skin off meat because I didn't want to eat the skin. This act finally fully divorced me from the idea of this chicken at one point being *a* chicken. Now it was chicken.

Be sure to discard the skin.

In his column, Roger Cohen writes of the moment he finally felt at home after moving to France as the moment when he saw glistening fish guts being coaxed by the ungloved hand of a friend from the belly of a sea bass. For Cohen, this moment, this image, represented the relationship between food and people that French culture has managed to preserve, while American food has been sanitized to the point of complete disconnect.

For me, this moment of reconnection, of realization, came when I held the freshly skinned and trimmed part of the chicken known as the tender in my palm. As a child, a white-blonde, freckled girl of the Northeast who refused to eat almost anything that remotely resembled an animal, refused to eat clams unless extracted, who never touched an oyster or a shrimp or a lobster, chicken tenders were my eating-out best friend. No matter where we were—even at the gritty-with-sand shack on the coast of New Hampshire's Hampton Beach, where food comes in cardboard boxes and customers sit at damp picnic tables over a concrete floor—I could get chicken tenders. But I had always assumed they were named "tenders" because of the shape, or the way of cooking them or something. I had no idea, until that day, until that moment, at age twenty-six, that the tender was actually a part of the chicken.

Once I had deboned the breast of the chicken and slid the meat apart from the body, the directions instructed me to slice along the thin white tendon that separated the breast from the tenders, the small plump flaps of flesh running along the edge of each breast. After I completed one side, I lifted the tender, puzzled, closer to my face for examination. Yup. Looked just like the breaded, deep-fried kind I'd eaten for the first eleven years of my life. I couldn't believe how perfect the meat looked, Easter-egg pink, the exact length of my palm. I laid the tender across my hand to poke and prod for a few more minutes.

I actually wandered around the apartment holding the tender, examining it, cradling it with the fleshy parts of my hand, utterly in awe.

My first encounter with the insides of a chicken had exactly the opposite effect I imagined it would. Rather than making me sick or grossing me out, rather than making me feel guilty or reaffirming my abandoned vegetarianism, seeing the anatomical realities of the chicken I would later eat gave way to a wonder I never expected. This was like the first time I saw the desperately grabbing tentacles on the bottom of a starfish, or a mosquito suck blood in time-lapse slow motion. I *got* it. Once I got under the skin and saw the veins, the tendons, the bones, the heart, I felt an indescribable attachment to the chicken that allowed me to accept it for what it was—a once-living animal, now dead, converted to food.

I still didn't cook the chicken for dinner that night. I decided I needed some space between the up-close examination and eating. But the next night, when I unwrapped the drumsticks from the aluminum foil in which I'd stored them, when I let them soak in buttermilk, then dredged them in egg and flour and laid them on a rack to bake, I swelled with pride. This was *my* chicken, a chicken I did more than buy, a chicken I'd known intimately, a chicken I'd approached full on. And later, when I held the ball of the drumstick in my hand and bit off the chewy dark flesh, I could honestly conjure, without gagging, the image of the dancing leg moving back and forth just before I dislocated it. The familiar pleasure of that memory mingled in my mouth with the distinctive moist taste of the chicken seasoned with mustard and hot sauce, and I swear, it really did taste better.

Chapter Twelve

Definitely Not June Cleaver

I **STOOD IN THE** middle of my kitchen with a potholder in one hand and a spatula in the other, and burst into tears. I gazed at the brown thing, burnt around the edges, soggy and droopy with chicken gravy—my first piecrust. A total culinary failure. My mind flooded with memories of rock-solid chocolate tortes and mashed potato messes from my youth. To the horror of my internal feminist, I found myself sobbing in the kitchen, thinking, *What good am I if I can't do this?*

I'd taken up buying and cooking food ethically with such a strong sense of purpose—this wasn't a lifestyle; this was a mission. I wanted to better care for the people I loved and the planet. I wanted to live better. And this was turning out to be a lot of pressure. Maybe I couldn't do it. I'd never been a good cook, had never followed through on so many of my activist dreams. Maybe, I thought, I am just an inherently bad cook, too distracted for domestication, too clumsy for the culinary arts, too feminist to be any good in the kitchen.

I'd spent so much of my life avoiding the kitchen, thinking of it as an oppressive space, the domestic realm to which women had, for so long, been condemned. And suddenly, I was spending all of my time there.

EVERY TUESDAY AFTERNOON, as summer faded into my second fall in Iowa, I stumbled home from my weekly pickup from the community-supported agriculture (CSA) cooperative I had joined with my arms full of fresh produce. Potatoes and yellow onions; raspberries, apples, red and green bell peppers. Blue plastic bags of leeks the length of my arm, their bulbous white roots still smelling of soil. A small bundle of baby bok choy, flowering green leaves wrapped with a blue rubber band. Knobby zucchini and summer squash, curved like elbows. A wealth of tomatoes, all heirloom varietals, some purple, striped, and bursting at the seams, others smaller and softer, sunset orange and golden yellow.

I had never eaten a tomato whose name I didn't know. I had never cooked a summer squash. I didn't even know which parts of a leek you could cook. But I was ready to try. Although I had never before thought I could, had never even really wanted to, I was becoming a cook.

What opened my eyes to my ability to manage in the kitchen, what awakened in me the possibilities inherent in food, was starting to eat meat again.

The more I learned about the food industry, the more I saw what I wanted to avoid. I realized the dangers of industrial agriculture were not just the restrictions of a pig's gestation crate or the environmental pollution of the salmon farming industry but also the bisphenol A lining the cans of green beans I'd sometimes buy or the color agents added to instant microwaveable rice. Preservatives, additives, chemicals, and subsidies all seemed as worrying to me as slaughter practices and animals' living conditions. The more I saw, the more I wanted to see. No longer did I focus only on eating humane meat. Now, I cared about eating humane, low-impact, healthy food, and for the most part, that meant making it myself.

I spent an hour or more preparing dinner every night. I researched ingredients on the Internet, Googling strange combinations. I pureed summer squash into a velvety-smooth soup, harvest sweet with just the right hint of salt, served with homemade Parmesan phyllo triangles. I roasted zucchini with bell peppers in balsamic glaze. I julienned bok choy and carrots into a homemade lo mein. I invented new pasta sauces based on the ingredients the season gave me: lemon sauce with sugar snap peas, creamy onion sauce dyed pink from the stems of rainbow chard. Every new experiment became a notch on my apron string, an achievement of which I felt genuinely proud.

But sometimes I tripped over my clumsy, undomesticated feet, trying too hard to create something new. When I got those first leeks in my CSA basket, I tried to adapt a recipe for a leek and sweet potato galette, with a combination of regular baking potatoes, orange peppers, and Gruyère cheese. I have no idea what I was thinking—perhaps that since the ingredients were of similar color, they would work together? Suffice it to say, they did not, and the bitterness of the leeks overpowered every other strange addition. A new reality began to set in. At first, proud of my ethical omnivore diet, reveling still in the high of new love, I was happy to take it on. But as the weather turned colder, I wondered how much time I was prepared to spend like this, how significantly this new diet would tether me to the kitchen.

ONE OF MY favorite vegetarian indulgences, usually only allowed on nights when I was home alone, no roommates or boyfriend around to judge, was a frozen Amy's single-serving vegetable potpie. The small aluminum container fit perfectly in the palm of my hand. I wore my sweat pants and ate my favorite comfort food, enjoying the familiarity of brown country gravy, warm whole wheat piecrust, and small cubes of tofu baked beside tiny white potatoes, peas, and corn. Naturally, when I started eating chicken again, I felt an immediate desire to bake a chicken potpie. But instead of buying a frozen potpie, I decided to make one from scratch, an endeavor that had never even occurred to me as a vegetarian—why would it when I could just go to the frozen foods section of the grocery store and grab one that came in a box? And I figured as long as I was peeling and dicing the potatoes and carrots, as long as I was hand-snapping fresh green beans off a stem, as long as I was simmering stock into homemade gravy, I might as well try making my own whole wheat piecrust, too. I'd made cookies and cupcakes here and there—how hard could a piecrust be?

I took an entire Friday afternoon to try to get it right. I cut butter into wheat pastry flour, bent over a white plastic bowl, slicing insistently as tiny crumbles began to form, little peas of butter encased in flour. I sprinkled water conservatively across the dough, and when it didn't stick, I dug my palms in to knead it together. The flour remained dry and loose, the water creating only tiny pockets of dough. I added more water, and more again. Finally, the dough formed into enough of a ball that I could turn it out onto the counter, pressing with my thumbs to connect the elastic dough, using the heels of my hands, hard, to work the gluten. Every knead clung to my palms, making me look like some yeasty swamp monster. I grabbed the rolling pin and slowly began to shape the sticky dough into a circle. Its edges cracked and peeled, falling away from itself.

I pressed on, undeterred, and laid the first heavy crust in the bottom of a pie dish, where it split right down the middle. I dabbed some water onto the crust to stick it back together, then filled it with the simmering gravy, shredded chicken, and vegetables. I quickly slid the other half-inch thick crust across the top. The two crusts were already too hard to even press the edges together, but I threw the whole thing on a cookie sheet and stuck it in the oven.

When I removed the pie from the oven, twenty minutes later, I set off the smoke alarm because so much gravy had seeped out over the unsealed edges and burned onto the floor of the oven. It took the heavy-duty serrated knife to cut two slices from the pie, both of which broke and slid off the spatula before making it to the plate. All that remained in the pie dish was a crumbling crust soaking in a pool of gravy. This was definitely not how June Cleaver's potpie would have turned out.

THE QUESTION I faced that fall was: Did cooking make me less of a feminist? *Of course not,* I thought—on the surface. Feminism is about choice, and as long as I'm the one choosing to do this, as long as it's what I truly want, there's nothing wrong with a feminist spending time in the kitchen.

But what I wanted wasn't so simple: I wanted to contribute to the local food system, but I hadn't really known that was going to necessitate so much cooking. I hadn't realized how much of myself I would invest in these meals, how much they would come to symbolize me, how proud I would be of each success, how much I would crumble with each failure. And how could I be sure of my own desires? I thought I wanted to cook, but I also wanted to wear a size two and have hair that looked like Jennifer Aniston's—not all desires are created equal. Some of what we want is born not of ourselves but of external pressure. Was my desire to cook, especially for my boyfriend, just social conditioning?

What if this notion of ethical eating and cooking was simply a way to justify walking down the path of traditional womanhood? Was I falling prey to some subconscious lure of domesticity?

This was the realm of femininity I'd tried to avoid when I'd stayed home with my father instead of joining my mother and sisters for girls' nights out, and suddenly, I could see the future playing out just the way I'd always feared. I was going to accidentally become a housewife, whistling cheerfully while I cooked my man a hot meal, grateful for a smack on the ass before he settled down in front of the television, while I ironed his work shirts and put the kids to bed, then pounded a couple of dirty martinis and a handful of mommy's little helpers.

I was spiraling. I was spiraling and I knew it. Nevermind that my mother wasn't some put-upon housewife, nevermind that she managed a career, nevermind that she loved cooking— this didn't feel right. I didn't feel like me. I didn't understand how I had ended up here, a woman, back in the kitchen, crying over the damned piecrust.

WHEN I LOST it, crying there in the kitchen over the sorry, sagging piecrust, Scott came over to comfort me, which in this case meant changing the subject. He wouldn't let me talk about the piecrust, or look at it. He firmly removed the spatula from my hands and steered me towards the door, out towards the yoga class I was already dressed to attend. On the drive there, I realized why I had become so upset: because I was cooking *for* someone, for him. Knowing that another person relied on me to be the good cook, to provide him with something other than ramen and pizza and peanut butter and jelly sandwiches meant I had no room to fail. This is what I had been afraid of as a girl, when I saw the power my mother and grandmother brought into the kitchen. Cooking as a gesture of love meant that failing to cook well could be equated with not loving enough.

And it was this thinking, this burden that was unfeminist. It wasn't my cooking that was a result of social pressures but rather seeing cooking as an obligation. Finding a way to blame myself for not being a better cook, thinking it was a duty or responsibility, was patriarchal conditioning. But I didn't have to succumb to it.

In yoga class that night, I stretched my hips backwards into downward-facing dog and tried to remind myself that all this was new territory for me. I remembered, as I moved into a warrior sequence, the strength I had felt in rising to the challenge of new ingredients, the kitchen muscles developing with every attempt and every failure. I was taking charge of the source of my food and doing the hard work of living ethically. Lying on my back and easing into final relaxation, I acknowledged that I wouldn't have been so upset by the piecrust if Scott hadn't been there. I breathed in. Truth is, I was embarrassed, wounded in a woman place, disappointed with myself for even having that place. I breathed out. Ultimately, this was my journey. The adventure of cooking, the experiments and failures, were mine. I had to claim my self as part of my mission, to accept that cooking was a gesture of love towards me, first and foremost.

Food could be a source of power, but only if I didn't let it control me. There was nothing to be afraid of, no failure big enough to cry over. I would try hard to be good, and laugh when I floundered. This was the difference between what I was doing and the housewife stereotype I imagined: growing into my own kitchen, finding a path that could both honor and expand upon the generations before me. I could take pride in joining my family's tradition of great women cooks, carrying down recipes and taking care of my family by feeding them well, *and* I could be an activist, serving chemical-free meals crafted from local, organic ingredients, food that came up out of the ground. I could be both radical and traditional. Even if that sometimes meant ordering takeout when I blew the homemade piecrust.

Chapter Thirteen

Precocious Squash

RIPPLING, GREEN SOUTHWESTERN Wisconsin ridges stretched towards a distant tree line, surrounding the tiny
yellow guesthouse where I would spend the next two
weeks. On a nearby rise sat a red packing barn and a wandering
black cat. This was Shooting Star, a small family-owned organic
vegetable farm run by husband and wife Rink and Jenny, who
had willingly accepted my offer to volunteer, in any capacity,
for the sake of getting closer to the source.

In the middle of my first spring as a meat eater, I'd gotten
comfortable with my cooking. I made biweekly pickups from
the CSA for fresh produce and had joined a local meat-buying
club, placing monthly orders for chicken, pork, and beef from
a variety of Iowa farms. But I was still in graduate school, and
between teaching two classes, taking three, and working on
my thesis, a book about my journey through local food, I didn't
have a lot of time to get out onto the farms I was buying from
and writing about.

Luckily, because of its environmental focus, my graduate program required a fieldwork component, which meant at some point during my summer off, I would need to find an environmental internship or volunteer experience as part of my course of study—ideally one that contributed to my developing thesis project. I knew this was the perfect opportunity to dig in more deeply, to get my hands dirty, to participate in the food system, but I didn't know where to look or how to begin.

One afternoon, I stopped by the office of one of my graduate professors, Dean, to brainstorm fieldwork ideas.

"I don't know." I shrugged. "What, do I just go work on a farm?"

Dean smiled. "Let me call my friend Rink."

Before moving to Iowa the past fall to teach at my university, Dean had spent ten years living in the small Wisconsin town of Mineral Point, a tight-knit community about forty miles from Madison, where he had befriended close to everyone. But he was especially close to Rink and Jenny. After a brief phone call with Dean and a few email exchanges, my two-week volunteer stay was arranged.

I'D NEVER IMAGINED myself working on a farm, but as I dug deeper into a meat-eating existence, I kept craving more information, more knowledge, more direct contact with the sources of my food. I sensed that the closer I got to the beginning—the seed, the soil, the farmer—the more I would understand.

Rink and Jenny bore some of the physical characteristics I'd expected from farmers: brushed-red cheeks from days of sun, plain and practical hair, easy to stuff under a hat or pull back in a rubber band. Both wore jeans, simple gray T-shirts, slip-on shoes. We sat and chatted quietly in their living room, each with one evening glass of white wine, while their son, Charlie, slept upstairs.

With the land I could see surrounding their large farmhouse, and a few part-time seasonal workers, Rink and Jenny ran a fully certified organic operation and an organic produce direct-to-restaurant distribution businesses. I had some sense that farm work would be hard work, yes, but beautiful, in peaceful surroundings. I was eager to get started. When I woke early the next morning, slathered myself in sunscreen, donned my breathable army surplus sun hat and work gloves, and headed out into the fields to help harvest, wash, package, and plant, I got my crash course in being a small-scale organic farmer. The hard work I imagined was merely an illusion, an idea of work, compared to how my body felt at the end of that first day.

We began the morning hauling trays of tomato, pepper, and eggplant seedlings out of the greenhouse and into the sun. Jenny explained that the warm-weather crops, harvested in midsummer, can't go straight from the heated greenhouse into the ground, where in late May, they still have to contend with cold. They need to be exposed to that early-morning air for a few weeks. A bit of bite in the air helps them become hardy enough to handle the soil.

My upper arms already pulsing with heat, I headed into the far field with Rink to pick French Breakfast radishes, the size and shape of arthritic fingers but bright, happy pink and white, to bundle them for sale. For about two hours, we crawled along the dirt, slimy with morning dew, wrapping our palms around wet green leaves and pulling the vegetables up out of the soil, counting to ten, then tying them in a loose bunch—crawl, pull, crawl, pull, count to ten, twist, repeat. By the time we stood up in the radish plot, my knees were already swollen and stiff.

Then, we moved for another three hours into the hoop house, a sort of giant greenhouse in which plants grow in the ground but remain covered by a large, curved, hard plastic roof. We picked turnips, pulling by the stems and bundling them by size, the smallest no bigger than the tip of my noise, the largest the size of a fist. In the hoop house, I moved around in a seated position to give my sore knees a break but soon felt a searing warmth spreading across my lower back. Later that week, I would notice stretched, sore abdominals, from bending and lifting fifty-pound bags of fertilizer, and strained hamstrings, from the sideways lunges I did up and down the rows while laying pepper plants.

More surprising than the physical aches of work on the farm, though, was the hard-packed dirtiness of it. "Dirty" doesn't even begin to describe the layer of slick you get up to your knees crawling up and down the ground of a hoop house that's just recently been watered, or laying irrigation strips beneath a plastic tarp covering the eggplant plot. We all know what happens when water mixes with soil. What you might not know is what that combination does to even your sturdiest hiking boots when you step ankle-deep in it: sucks the shoe right off your foot, so that you come down into the muddy soil in nothing but a gym sock.

All that dirt and muck, the smudges of it on my face and arms, crusted into my braids, reminded me of the fundamental truth of the farm. Food grows in the ground, right up out of the dirt of the earth. And sometimes that's messy.

THE TOPIC OF lunchtime conversation—which would also be the topic of tomorrow's breakfast conversation, the topic of conversation every morning and every night here—was the weather. Every night, Jenny had a report about how much rain might be falling tomorrow, and during which hours. For maybe the first time in my life, this kind of information was not small talk but absolute necessity. Knowing that it would rain between one and three in the afternoon meant we had to get started an hour earlier to get all the lettuce harvested and out of the field before lunch, so that we could wash and pack in the barn during the showers. Cutting lettuce in the rain would make for slimy leaves that would take more washes to come clean, wilting the lettuce with too much moisture.

Jenny had to know the weather. She had to know when it was going to rain to plan the daily schedule, to decide whether or not to put the seedlings in the ground, to know if we'd need to water the baby lettuces waiting for harvest or if they would have a storm to help them grow for another two days in the warming June sun without drying out before they were ready to pick. Knowing the weather meant knowing how much produce would be for sale that week.

One afternoon late in the week, one of the part-time workers and I got caught in a torrential downpour while attempting to plant leeks, their newborn root structures disintegrating in our fingers, the seedling threads like blades of grass, crumbling with just the first few drops. We had to run inside to save them, soggy jeans slinging down around my hips, then eat avocado sandwiches standing up in the kitchen to avoid muddying the house. The weather was ever present, another reminder that food growing is an operation that requires nature's cooperation, a cycle that can't be complete without the basics of sunlight and water. A simple truth. But in the world of Taco Bell's 88 percent beef burrito, a world suburban and distant from soil, one easily forgotten.

LATE IN THE afternoon on my first day of work, Rink took me for a walk through the carefully planned fields of the farm's acre and a half to show me which crops occupied each plot. We stopped in front of a fallow plot, a patch of field that looked to me like a lawn cut for the first time, full of dead grasses lying sideways, uprooted, but nearly four feet long. Rink told me that just two days earlier, this had all been wheat, which they plant in rotation with their regular crops to regenerate soil nutrients. Saturday night, Rink said, just days before I arrived, the wheat had been tall enough that their son, Charlie, and some of his four-year-old playmates had chased each other through the tall, lush field, playing hide-and-seek. Now it lay dormant, Rink having tilled the remaining nubs of wheat over, so that it would slowly decay back into the soil.

"This is what I love about the farm," he told me. "It's ephemeral."

Although any given field looks different from one day to the next, Rink sees the whole farm as engaged in one endlessly repeating cycle, each field a demonstration plot of a different step along the same path from soil to seed to plate.

THE NIGHT I first arrived at the farm, I stayed up talking with Rink and Jenny about what I hoped to learn there, about getting closer to understanding the hands-on reality of the abstract food system, the path I had taken through seven years as a vegetarian to their doorstep. As soon as I mentioned that I was researching post-vegetarian food ethics, the two of them looked at each other, smiled, and told me I had to meet Bartlett.

Bartlett Durand was co-owner of Black Earth Meats, a fresh meat supply center in a nearby small town. A few days into my first week on the farm, I sat down for a two-hour chat with Bartlett over coffee. His brown hair cropped neat and short, Bartlett wore a white polo shirt tucked into his belted jeans and carried sharp sunglasses and a BlackBerry. He looked more the part of a suburban dad on the weekend than a sustainable food activist, but as we began to talk, I saw the ways in which his story mirrored mine. As a practicing Buddhist, he had been a vegetarian for many years, attempting to live his life by causing as little suffering as possible. But when he spent several years living in India, studying yoga and martial arts, the mental struggles of meditation took a physical toll on his body, and he began eating fish again, as a means of fueling his spiritual development and more closely engaging with the Hindu aspects of his geographic surroundings.

When Bartlett returned to Wisconsin, he struggled to find local, sustainable sources of meat that had been raised and slaughtered in ways he considered humane. When a local slaughterhouse announced its bankruptcy and closing, Bartlett and his father-in-law, Gary Zimmer, a pioneer of mineralized, balanced agriculture, bought the facility. Within a few years, Black Earth Meats was a fully developed meat supply chain, buying livestock animals directly from farmers willing to adhere to their strict and specific standards for living conditions, slaughtering them humanely, distributing the meat directly to restaurants and stores throughout the upper Midwest, and running a retail front right out of the slaughterhouse.

We'd spoken for a few hours and as our conversation wound down, I wanted to spend more time picking Bartlett's brain about the idea of humane slaughter. I'd spent a lot of time over the last year and a half thinking about how animals were raised and cared for, how livestock farmers found ways to respect and support the ecology of a farm and the local economy. But I still struggled with a central question, born out of my vegetarian past, born out of the PETA video that started this all: Was there such a thing as a kind way to kill? So I asked Bartlett if he could walk me through the process by which an animal was slaughtered at Black Earth Meats. I wanted to know the specifics of his ethical framework: How, exactly, did it look, feel, sound, to slaughter an animal humanely?

He handed me his card and said, "You know, it's just easier to see it yourself. Why don't you come watch?"

He told me they slaughtered every Wednesday morning, and I should stop by next week.

I was floored. I couldn't believe someone would just offer to let me in. He wanted me to see a slaughter. I didn't even have to ask.

SATURDAY MORNING, THE end of my first week on the farm, Rink and I started loading up the van around six: two fold-out tables; a couple of checkered cloths; plastic crates and bag-lined cardboard boxes full of arugula, red and green Bibb lettuces, turnips, radishes, spinach, rhubarb, and parsnips. We were headed for the market.

In wet pigtail braids and a long-sleeved shirt against the slight chill of the early morning in late Midwestern spring, I looked around Mineral Point's Water Tower Park, packed already with vendors and customers. I was terrified. As an introvert, I'd never been much a fan of interacting with strangers. I knew I'd have to do a lot of math in my head. Plus, I'd never worked a farmers market—or a farm—before. Rink and Jenny had been so kind to let me work for them, given that I was so utterly lost in the fields, and I was afraid of messing up. Market is a significant portion of their livelihood—no longer could I take things slow to avoid bundling too many shrimpy radishes, or to make sure to trim just the right amount of stem from the baby arugula I harvested. This was business.

Once we wrestled the canvas roof tent open and laid out the tablecloths, once we'd stacked crates of turnips in piles behind us and arranged flowering heads of red Bibb in a display, I began prepping bags of spinach. I quickly figured out that one of my loose handfuls was about two ounces of spinach and sped up, tossing handfuls of dewy leaves gently into plastic bags, trying to figure out how to subtract the weight of the plastic bag on the portable scale, and carefully folding the loose plastic over on itself for sale. After a few moments, lost in the comforting repetition of toss, tare, twist-tie, I looked up to see that the floodgates had opened. Just before nine, when the market officially opened, customers with cloth bags and red wagons, led by children or dogs, edged their ways up to our table and began shopping. I watched as food transformed yet another once-empty space into a community.

Although I expected to be working the farmers market that day, I hoped as behind the scenes as possible, what happened instead was that Rink spent the next few hours introducing me to everyone. Since Dean, my professor and friend, had once lived in Mineral Point, nearly every customer to Rink and Jenny's booth was an old friend. All Rink needed to say was "She knows Dean."

And the replies rolled in: people asking how Dean was as a teacher, telling me how much they missed him, lauding praise on the great work he did for the arts in Mineral Point, laughing over their favorite drinking-buddy story of him. We were selling food, but by the end of that morning, I felt more engaged with the town than I had in the week I'd spent there so far.

Near the end of the market, as business started dying down, Rink shooed me away from the booth. "Go explore," he said.

I wandered in laps around the park and watched as a small town affirmed its identity. Children climbed on the playground structures, half-eaten carrots and turnips dangling from their hands. A string band played polka. Amish men and dreadlocked women sold goods side by side. A new resident in town, someone's transplant wife, bought something from every table, as a way of introducing herself to the community.

On the drive back to the farm, Rink told me that in Mineral Point, they called market "church." This was their weekend worship ritual, their version of finding spirituality and living in harmony with a higher moral calling. Although it was sort of a joke—the market was a place for gossip and socializing, where people who lived ten miles out of town could catch up with their friends—there was a current of truth to the mingling of food and religion. On the cool, sunny afternoon I spent there, I couldn't conjure something more serious, something any heavier with good intentions than a community committing itself to supporting the people who worked hard to provide healthy, safe food for their neighbors' children. When hands were shaken and produce exchanged, it meant something greater. Something like: *Take this, all of you, and eat of it.*

THE FOLLOWING WEDNESDAY, I hugged Rink and Jenny and Charlie goodbye, and thanked them for letting me muck around in their farming business for a week. And at six in the morning, I drove through the lifting Wisconsin fog to Black Earth Meats. I was nervous, thinking back to that awful PETA video, and wondered if seeing a slaughter would put me off meat for good. But I also knew I couldn't not witness it. Watching the gruesome reality of an inhumane industrial slaughterhouse had been the reason I'd started boycotting meat. If I was going to eat meat again, if I was going to participate in the slaughter as a consumer, I needed to face that reality. I just hoped this slaughterhouse would look different than the one I'd seen all those years ago in Professor Bob's classroom.

I walked through the front door and told the woman working the counter that Bartlett said I could watch a slaughter. She nodded, then asked if I had brought boots. I hadn't—for some reason, proper footwear for a blood-soaked floor hadn't occurred to me—so she took me to an upstairs room, outfitted me with a pair of green rubber boots, a hairnet, a white coat. She didn't ask me any questions, let alone the one I was thinking: *Why are you here?* She simply led me onto the slaughter floor and introduced me to Francisco, the floor manager, and said, "Bartlett sent her." Nobody thought this was weird. Nobody found it strange that I wanted to watch. Nobody was cagey. There were no cameras or locked fences or security guards. No ID necessary. Nothing to hide.

It was here that my eyes opened fully: when I watched the invisible punch of the bolt gun invade the steer's head and saw it crumple to the ground, when I saw the dancing cheek of the dead steer, when I watched the sawing and skinning and slicing. And the whole time, I was standing beneath a sign that read *We Honor These Animals, for By Their Death, We Gain Life.*

WHAT I LEARNED at Shooting Star Farm was: it was really hard to be a farmer. You don't make enough money—Rink told me that he decided to work part time on the farm and part time for his own distribution business when he figured out he wasn't making full-time wages from his land. You had to put in long hours—nearly every night, either Rink or Jenny was back out in the fields after dinner, after Charlie's bedtime, watering or mowing or weeding. The work was painful. My back ached with radiating pain after just a few hours bending and straightening to put tomato seedlings in the ground. My knees split from crawling along soil and rock. My palms blistered from hoe-weeding.

You needed specialized knowledge about nature that most Americans abandoned generations ago, about weather patterns and rain collection and soil nutrient cycles. You had to jump through hoops—one day, Jenny spent five hours with the organic certification officer, for whom she organizes the farm's entire purchasing line, keeping years of receipts for everything from fertilizer to seedlings in labeled filing cabinets. He told her she had the best-organized system he'd ever seen. You have to do all this while raising your kid and working Saturdays.

But I also learned that they loved farming. Both Rink and Jenny came from non-farming backgrounds: Rink born and raised in Chicago, later a prep cook at Chez Panisse; Jenny on her way to a master's in psychology. They were tenant farmers at first, living in a one-room house with a sleeping loft on the land they planted until they could afford to buy it and build a full house. And still, on our tour of the farm the first day, Rink pulled back the plastic covering over one row of crops to reveal sprouting baby lettuces and asked, "Isn't that so pretty?" They loved this life. They chose it for themselves.

ON MY DRIVE back to Iowa, after leaving Black Earth Meats, I stopped when I saw a sign along the highway advertising the filming site for *Field of Dreams*. Just a few hours after watching a slaughter for the first time, I took tourist photos of an abandoned baseball diamond, a set of white wooden bleach-ers, a cornfield. I bought a souvenir T-shirt. I texted my father a photo, wrote, *Can you guess where I am? Hint: it's not heaven, just Iowa.*

I felt strange, even then, self-aware. Surely I was missing something. Why wasn't I affected more? Why hadn't I pulled off the side of the road to throw up? Why hadn't I cried? *I watched an animal die this morning,* I kept thinking. *Why don't I feel it?*

In the following weeks, when I told people the story of the slaughterhouse, and they asked about my emotional reaction, I used vague platitudes—"powerful," "moving," "significant"—to avoid admitting that the truth was: I didn't feel much. I couldn't figure it out. I walked into the slaughterhouse that day fully prepared to have a profound spiritual experience, to learn what it really meant that animals died for me to eat. But I didn't feel changed.

One lazy summer Saturday, a few weeks after returning from my stay at the farm, I settled in to watch the documen-tary *Food, Inc.* In the early moments of the film, the crew toured an industrial chicken house under contract with Tyson. The female chicken farmer walked among her birds, picking up the dead ones from where they'd collapsed under the weight of their own oversized bodies, tossing them into the lowered bucket of a bulldozer. The camera found one chicken in the process of dying, its broken legs kicking wildly, its massive chest rising and falling desperately, trembling with spasms, maybe a heart attack.

I burst into tears, right there on the couch of my apart-ment, miles and years away from this dying chicken. I thought back to Black Earth Meats, and then back further, to the PETA video that had started me on the path of vegetarianism. And

I understood why I didn't feel this sobbing, tearing sadness in the slaughterhouse: because there was no injustice to it.

At Black Earth Meats, I stood and watched, calm and accepting, because I saw only the simple reality: life, and then death.

But in the films, I saw death that should not have happened the way it did, death unfair.

The chickens in this film, the piglets in the PETA film, were disposable bodies, bodies that human hands treated as objects, not living things. The bodies suffered, for no real reason, with no real consequence—hardly anyone seemed to notice. Humans may never be able to fully understand animal suffering, whether they feel pain the same way we do, and whether that even matters to all of us, as eaters. We can abstract and theorize the neurology of consciousness, but the truth is, I know what pain looks like. Deep in my bones. I know what suffering is when I see it happen.

AND I KNOW the opposite: I can recognize genuine care, too.

On one of my last days at the farm, Rink and I walked up and down the rows, one foot in front of the other, tossing squash seedlings to the soil, where we would later crawl and scoop up palmsful of dirt to plant them.

Rink stopped, rested the tray of seedlings on his hip, and asked, "You know what I love about squash?"

I smiled and shook my head.

"It's so precocious," he said, returning to the rhythmic dropping.

What he meant was that squash plants flower very quickly, taking only about a week from the day we put them in the ground to blossom. To Rink, this plant was one of the best representations of the cyclical nature of a vegetable farm. But I was struck by how human he made them, how he described his plants with the same adjective people might use to describe their children. Rink doesn't love the plants the same way he loves his son, but he does love them, with the pride that comes from a powerful, long-term devotion. That's when I saw farming for what it meant to Rink and Jenny, slaughter for what it meant to Bartlett. More than hard work. More than sore knees and sunburns, more than extra paperwork and no spare cash for health insurance. More than disposable bodies, more, even, than death. Their life was farmers markets and shaking hands. Wind and sun and rain, the reason for soil. Honor and sacrifice. The nature of things. Pretty lettuce and precocious squash. As simple and beautiful as growing food for people to eat.

Chapter Fourteen

Elk Country, Part II

"**D**o you feel that?" Rick turned to me and asked, tucking the brim of his camouflage cap up an inch on his forehead. "How everything just got quieter?"

I nodded, silently, solemnly, though I was lying. I had not felt the quiet. I'd been focusing on the trail in front of me, which was particularly rocky here, and on the way my brand-new hiking boots slipped over the shards of mountain slick with pine needles and a slight lingering frost. I hadn't been listening. I'd just been trying to keep up. He pointed to the ground.

"This is the imaginary dotted line in the woods. When I cross it, I'm in elk country."

The morning hadn't yet begun when we headed out, pulling on gear in the empty trailhead parking lot, loading the rifle by headlamp shine. I'd stumbled along the first few miles of the marked trail in darkness, skipping to keep up with the brisk pace set by someone who had done this many times before and hoping my rain pants swishing as my thighs moved rapidly weren't making too much noise. The sun rose gradually over the next few hours. Deep in the crease of a canyon in south-western Montana, surrounded on all sides by glacier-cut rock and centuries-old pines, the sunrise appeared to me only as a slow graying of the air I breathed, dark purple giving way to the fuzzed pale fog of daylight in the mountains. Gray gave an ethereal, hushed quality to the day, the sounds of our boots muffled by a carpet of needles, one of the only sounds the occasional swish of a branch against our jackets.

As we walked the first few miles, he told me about how hunting had changed for him. He told me it used to be an adrenaline thing, a got-to-get-that-animal drive of problem solving, a heart-pounding urgency, a competition. Most of it was gone now for him, he said, and he missed it. Now, it was as much about being in the woods and walking around as it was about taking an animal.

I still couldn't believe I was here. I couldn't believe this was really happening. It had only been one week ago that Rick had agreed to let me accompany him on this hunt, and only a few weeks earlier that the idea had been planted in my mind. I was sitting in a graduate classroom, workshopping the essay I'd written about my time on the farm, when my thesis advisor, Ben, said, "I know how your book ends. You hunting elk in the woods of Montana."

Ben suggested Montana partially because he knew I'd lived there, and had written about hunting culture in the state before, but also because he knew a writer, Rick, who lived in Montana and was also a mindful and ethical hunter. It was both a literary and a practical suggestion. The more I thought about it, the more I realized how right Ben was: the hunt was something I needed to see. Again, something I'd never expected to find myself doing materialized as a possibility and crystallized quickly. Just days after his initial comment, I was in Ben's office, asking if he could really make it happen.

Convincing Rick wasn't easy. As many of us writers do, Rick preferred his time alone. But beyond that, the act of hunting was a private affair, an intimate connection between him, the animal, and the woods. Which was exactly the reason I wanted to join him, and not just anyone, on a hunt. I didn't want to see how the average American meat eater might hunt. I wanted to observe someone who I knew respected the land and the animal. When I explained that to him, he agreed; he was free, he said, next weekend. I used up all my frequent flyer miles and booked a round-trip ticket to Missoula.

The weekend I arrived in Montana, in early October 2010, the local university was hosting a book festival, so the night before our planned hunt, Rick invited me out to a dinner where he and a crowd of other writers were gathered. When I arrived, I squeezed into a corner seat, separated from him by a dozen or so people. After a few minutes, he came around the table to crouch beside me, among the crowd, to hash out our plans for the next morning. I sensed he was testing me.

When I said, "I just want to see what it means to hunt," I could see in the softening of his face, in his solemn nod, that I'd said the right thing.

Later, when we thought for a while the hunt was over, and we were walking straight down a steep ridge to find our way back to the hiking trail, he turned and said, "We're not really hunting right now. We're just walking."

WE LEFT THE trail about four miles in, veered off to the right, and headed straight up a steep, rocky slope. The debris grew slicker as we climbed, and he told me this was how he knew there'd be snow up ahead. We cut back and forth across the mountain, lungs heaving, arms slicing through snapping branches, ankles turning as our feet slid from rock to uneven soil. We were going to climb long and high, he'd told me already, to come down into the burned remains of the canyon from the north, so that the animal—that's how he spoke of it, as a single one, the mythic, iconic animal—wouldn't catch our scent on the southern wind.

As we scaled—or as he scaled, and I scrambled up behind him—and our bodies leaned into the incline, my hands sometimes dusting the frosty soil in front of me for balance, he would pause, his voice hushed now as the sun bore through our heavy jackets, and crouch slightly, pointing towards a patch of scuffed dirt where he spotted clusters of pellets, or hoofprints.

"There. An animal."

When he showed me the signs of the animal, I could see them, but if he hadn't been there, I never would have known. He was tuned to the higher frequency of the hunter.

I knew this wouldn't be the day I learned to stalk an elk. Why had I ever thought it could be taught in only one day? This was a lifetime's work, to learn the woods.

AS WE CLIMBED up the hard stone flats, I thought back to when I'd lived here in Montana and about Maggie, my coworker from the gift shop who told me she couldn't be friends with a vegetarian. It had been five years since then, and I was no longer making the black-and-white distinction between the ethics of meat eating versus vegetarianism. I felt myself edging closer to understanding what hunting meant to her, though it wasn't until I was out there, in the woods with Rick, that I felt for myself how bonding this experience could be.

I thought of my own family. Perhaps it was because of the clarity the vast outdoors afforded, or the deep connection I was trying to forge with hunter and hunted, but I had the most vivid memory of standing in my family's crowded kitchen, after a long day of making pasta in steaming copper-bottomed pots, the pasta rolling in the boils of the water. I imagined Gampi teaching my sisters and me how to test its doneness, how to tell when the pasta had reached al dente perfection. Maggie's father taught her to skin an animal with the hand-carved knife he had given her for her thirteenth birthday, a lesson not unlike the one I learned over pasta, watching Gampi turn the hand crank on the pasta machine. It was the slow process of watching food become. I understood, somehow, why my family was so unnerved when I became a vegetarian. *This is not how I taught you to feed yourself.*

Years ago, the antler barrettes Maggie made with her father made me cringe, but now I see in them how close she was to her food. For so long, I'd lost that connection, the thoughtfulness I wanted to bring to my own eating. I now knew there were migrant workers doing backbreaking work for pennies to ship vegetables to my supermarket and synthetic chemicals in my vegetarian food. I'd seen other people elbow-deep in making food from animal bodies, and it didn't scare me. It seemed Maggie's approach to food wasn't so different than mine after all. For both of us, it was about the people, the connection, the respect for the origins or our food and the art that went into making meals.

This hunt, I knew, my breathing growing heavier, could be more than sport, more than a desire to pull a trigger, more than a greedy lust for death. There was something honest about it: being unafraid to get messy, the admission that it was all messy, touching the heart of the food chain.

WHEN WE STOPPED for lunch, brushing snow off a log near the side of the slope we were climbing, my exhaustion began to set in. My ears rang with the thump of exertion; my cheeks were flushed with blood. I crouched on the log and ate peanut butter and jelly ravenously, to quell the light-headedness, and Rick showed me how much farther we had to go. From here, we could see the canyon, and he pointed down into it, to a patch of blackened trees that had burned years before. There, where the elk made their day beds, high enough to ensure a thick blanket of snow cooled them as they slept, we'd find the bull he was after.

The climb became harder. Suddenly aware of my awkwardness, I heard every branch that snapped under my feet; I flushed with embarrassment at the noisiness of my labored breathing. Rick pulled ahead of me easily while I willed my legs to *lift* in and out of the now ankle-deep snow. He stopped and told me I was doing great—for someone who'd come from sea level. I was hauling myself up by tree trunks and seeing little hypnotic worms around the edges of my vision, when I saw that he'd stopped up ahead.

"There they are." Elk tracks.

And that's when we heard the gunshot.

"SHIT. FUCK."

Our eyes met, our faces static and waiting. No second shot. He swore again, under his breath, turning from me slightly.

"That was our animal."

I was following him blindly through the woods, but his path had been intentional—he'd been following a single bull elk this whole time, tracing its visible path through the trees in the scuffs of dirt and hoofprints in the snow. He knew it was one animal. He even thought, having hunted this herd in these woods before, that he knew exactly which bull elk we were following. But now it was clear that another hunting party had entered the woods from another direction, and had beat us to the animal we'd spent the whole morning tracking.

We hiked on a little, following the now easy-to-spot hoofprints in the snow. Soon, the prints of another animal, a horse, danced in and out of the elk's to form a wide, woven trail, something more obtrusive than anything I'd seen all day, obvious, the way it is when people walk in snow.

"In all the years I've been hunting around here, I've never seen another soul, not one person," he said.

We heard the whinny of a distant horse. He showed me where the elk had first noticed it wasn't alone, how the prints began to weave around trees, up and down the slope. He laughed and shook his head, as if at an old friend's joke, a familiar, endearing story. The elk was toying with them.

As we walked, I placed my feet intentionally in the elk's trail, treading the same path as a dead or dying animal, as if walking in its footsteps would help me understand something.

Just down the ridge slightly, Rick began waving, seeing the hunting party before I did. He swore under his breath again and then called, cheerful, "Congratulations!"

I must have looked crazy to them, in my heavy rain pants and fleece vest beneath my winter coat, a hat pulled down around pigtail braids and black smudges of burned tree char on my face from where I'd tried to wipe the sweat clear with dirtied hands. When I saw them, I saw the hunters I'd always imagined, the men with cowboy hats and blaze orange vests, who rode in on horseback and photographed themselves with casual arms draped over the broken neck of a newly dead animal. The one with the blue sweater, who'd fired the fatal shot, held a small hatchet meant for butchering, spread his arms wide, and said, "Welcome to my kill."

I remember the enormity of the animal, and the faint stuffy smell of its fur, damp with sweat and snow. I remember seeing the puddle of blood and thinking, *This is where it all was*. I remember its open brown eyes, wet with the glaze of death. I watched carefully its rear haunch, its massive chest cavity, not yet split open, fully expecting the lungs to heave once more, a hoof to kick a last-ditch effort at life.

I had never been closer to the source of my food. This was a far cry from a frozen, lab-created, fake MorningStar Chik'n. This was all blood, all body, all sweat and death. The body was still, as if in surrender. We left the three men to clean and pack the elk, and carry it out on horseback.

THE NATIVE AMERICAN tribes of the Great Plains are sometimes called the "buffalo tribes," because the animal was so central to every aspect of their way of life.[1] Although some tribes were fully nomadic, following the herds along their seasonal paths of migration, and others were semisedentary, raising crops in addition to hunting bison, all relied on the bison for food, clothing, shelter, decoration, crafting, and spirituality. Before the tribes fully adopted horse culture in the early eighteenth century, they hunted and killed bison on foot, requiring large numbers of indigenous hunters to move out early, surround a bison herd, and drive it into a place where the animals could be most easily slaughtered.

Sometimes the tribes would build V-shaped funnels and corral the bison into an enclosed space where they could be easily targeted with bow and arrow. A hunter dressed in the preserved skin of a bison, imitating the call of the animal, could induce a stampede, and then direct the flow of snorting, startled animals directly off a cliff, where sometimes hundreds of bison would fall to their deaths.

As we left the small band of men, hunting, then eating, together, I was reminded of those first lonely nights in D.C., early on in my vegetarianism, when I sat on the couch alone in the glow of the television, eating food products from multiple packages. What a strange distance between the source and the food. How alone I was then.

A pack. A herd. Where was mine?

I guess I strayed from my pack because I no longer ate like them, but growing up, my family had certainly eaten in a herd-like manner. Although our kitchen table was enormous, it still was not big enough to fit the whole lot of us around it. It was like that painting hanging on the wall above the table in my childhood kitchen, the framed print of Norman Rockwell's *Freedom from Want.*

The pack feasted together.

Here, the hunters were bowing their bodies over the animal that had died for them to eat. They were speaking to their food—the butchery an act of thanks.

Rick knew the rest of the herd would have panicked hearing the gunshots, charging down the mountain to their safe, familiar bedding spots. He knew another kill was impossible today. With the echo of a gunshot fresh in their animal brains, they wouldn't let their guard down easily. And I was showing my exhaustion, dizzy and panting. We decided to begin the hike out.

We descended along the nose of the ridge, across the elk's canyon from our lunch spot, weaving back and forth out towards the edge, where Rick had once seen his favorite, the prized big bull, bedded down. We followed the small herd's frantic tracks away from the kill site—great swathes of dirt kicked up, paths staggering, intersecting, careening away from each other. Even I could see this. He showed me where some more surefooted, older elk had found well-known escape routes, and where young, flustered elk had just spooked, knowing only that they should run down.

Elk were once plains animals, he told me as we hiked out. They roamed the Great Plains alongside bison and other herd grazers. So they were grass animals, flat land animals. But white settlers moved onto the plains and needed more and more land for themselves, tearing up grasses to plant fields, or to build houses, and the elk were forced farther west until they had no choice but to move up into the mountains. Their bodies developed thicker skin, heavy with fur. Their hooves hardened, their bones strengthened into a tougher skeleton, to better weather the tough climbs and treacherous stumbles of a ridge and canyon life. And their herds shrunk, because there is so much less grass on a mountain's stiff vertical incline, too little grass to support multiple elk families. Now, they grazed in herds of four or five, just cows and calves, with bulls ranging separately. Despite the best efforts of geography and evolution, the elk couldn't shake their communal lifestyle. No matter how small their numbers, they still roamed in small herds.

HALFWAY DOWN THE ridge we were descending, Rick stopped. He'd pulled the rifle up to his shoulder so many times, I didn't think much of it anymore—except he fired it this time, and the gunshot rang like it'd been fired in my skull. I watched, distracted, as the golden shell dropped to the soil, and didn't get my hands up to my ears for the second shot, either.

When he turned to see if I'd spotted the animal, his face broke into a wide grin at the shock in my expression. He spoke more softly than he had all day, told me we'd have to sit and wait. I was puzzled but compliant, though thoughts burst into my mind and I wanted suddenly to talk, to run over what had happened, what we'd each seen. But instead, we waited in excruciating silence, so that the animal wouldn't hear us and try to run. If it was wounded, we wanted it to lie down and die right there. We wanted the death to be fast and painless. We wanted the elk to be easier to track to the kill site.

We hadn't been looking. I hadn't even seen the animal. We froze, and he fired, twice.

WHEN I READ accounts of pre-colonial plains bison hunts, I am struck by how similar they sound to the large-scale nineteenth-century hunts of European colonizers. There may not have been gunshots or horses, but we can imagine that the bison were equally startled, to be willing to stampede off a cliff. We can assume a level of fear. I couldn't know whether it was more or less painful or desirable to be killed by a bullet wound or by smashing my skull on a cliff floor, my brain exploding out from inside. Why, then, did it feel different? The weapons and circumstances may have been different, but the fates of the animals were essentially the same—the bison ended up dead in both stories.

The difference for me lay within what happened afterwards, in the results of the Native Americans bison hunts. To get optimum use out of the animal, the Native Americans had a specific method of butchering, skinning down the back in order to get at the tender meat just beneath the surface. Then the front legs would be cut off, along with the shoulder blades, to expose the hump meat as well as the meat of the ribs and the bison's inner organs. After everything was exposed, the spine was severed and the pelvis and hind legs removed. Finally, the neck and head were removed as one. This allowed for the tough meat to be dried and made into pemmican, a mixture of fat and protein that was more easily preserved. In this way, each bison rendered as much meat as possible, enough to last a family an entire winter. After all this, the hunters would tan the hide for leather to sew into clothing and tipis, strip the sinew for bows, scoop out the fat and innards for cooking grease, dry the dung to build fires, and even boil the hooves for glue.

This in-depth processing may have just been reality—certainly these practices evolved from necessity of life on the plains. But there was a ceremony to it, the ritual of processing an animal so thoroughly as to become respectful. Maybe this suggested that the idea of *how* an animal dies was not limited simply to the conditions of its life, or to the process of the hunt, or to the circumstances of its death, but also to the aftermath. In order to fully own the reality of an animal dying for human consumption, perhaps we have to be willing to dig our hands in after the fact, to muddy around in the blood and sinew long enough, to understand the possibilities inherent in its body. By refusing to leave any part of the animal behind, the plains tribes honored the animal's sacrifice, venerating its life enough to make good use of its death.

While Rick and I sat and waited, I began to process what I had seen today. The way the hunt illuminated the connection between food and body. The blood pounding in our ears. How the elk's blood was transformed, through the conscious acts of butchery into the tenderloin and steak of a meal. There was little barrier between human and food.

I imagined my great-grandmother's hands rolling meatballs and remembered the wine we used to make in grandparent's backyard. I recalled the feeling of grapes being pulverized underfoot and the faintest purple juice staining me up to my ankles. A process from beginning to table, gorgeous and grotesque, to ingest something that had slimed its way up your ankles and elbows.

When it was time, we found the spot he'd shot the elk marked by a surprisingly small amount of blood. We weren't in snow, having descended far enough to come out of it for a while, and we had to find and follow the blood trail to the animal across rocks and pine needles and fallen tree branches.

Finally, I had a hunting skill: I could spot the blood trail with ease. For some reason, I could easily see the small splotches and smears of red against the forest's browns and greens. We crept, hunched over, staring intensely at the forest floor, and I would spin my head slowly, point: "Here's some." And revel in his surprised "Jesus," because I could finally contribute to the hunt. No longer just a spectator, I was part of this, the careful stalking.

We wove improbably around, watching for blood smears on sagging trees, as the trail looped back over itself. Clearly, the animal was panicked—a sign, Rick thought, that it may have lain down nearby. But after a few moments, he began muttering again. This wasn't nearly enough blood. Worst-case scenario. A nonfatal shot.

Sometimes we had to touch a spot to test whether that was a speckle of blood on a leaf or just the orange of fall beginning to pull the chlorophyll from the plant. Blood. I rubbed the familiar warmth between my fingertips, brushed it off onto my pants, staining them for good. Every now and then there would be a lurch, a gap in the steady but minuscule stream of blood. In one spot, Rick found bone—a fragment of leg or shoulder that told him the bullet had ricocheted inside the animal's body, the shot probably not direct enough to reach any vital organs—and swore again.

After what felt like an hour, we hit snow and found a giant puddle, a wide ribbon of bright red blood. I was sure we'd find a body any moment and was already dreading the weight of meat slung around my shoulders. But no. The elk had started to give in, had lain and rolled in the cold snow, and then had surged, with a last burst of life, to its feet. A few paces away, there was another, smaller puddle where the elk had fallen again. But again, it had kept going.

WHEN I SAW the blood of the elk on my fingertips, I understood that I could no longer turn away from the fact that animals die for us to eat. Even if we don't consume flesh, we can't look away from the implications our actions have in the pursuit of this death. Vegetarians who purchase meat substitute products are simply eating a different product made by multinational corporations that also raise and kill livestock. Even a small-scale, organic, family-owned vegetable farm uses natural methods to kill off pests. If we acknowledge that we are a part of a web of life, we must acknowledge that any action we take to feed ourselves is inherently disruptive to that web. To look away is to abdicate responsibility. Ignoring the death of the bison is to ignore our own death, to forget that we are all still animals, caught in an intricate web of survival, a complex dance about the quality of an animal's life, the conditions and dignity of a death.

SEVEN YEARS AFTER I gave up meat, there I was, standing behind a man in the mountains of Montana while he fired two rounds through the trees into the body of an elk. I crept around the woods with him, our fingers tracing over pine needles and fallen trees, brushing through the blood trail leading us on. I sat and rested on the side of a canyon ridge while he pressed on, half-jogging deeper into the crevice of rock as the light faded fast, desperate to find the animal and finish the kill. I saw his face when he glanced back and forth between the purpling sky and the disappearing trail, and watched the devastation draw down across his expression as he was forced to admit the ugly reality that he hadn't killed the animal. He had only wounded it.

After the two puddles, the blood virtually disappeared, and Rick told me what the elk had actually been doing in the snow was packing its wound. Instinctive first aid. Animals knew to roll around in snow to stop the bleeding. He stood in front of me, in Carhartt outdoor wear and a camouflage hat, rifle in hand, heartbroken to have to leave a wounded animal alive. Not because he wanted the meat, or the thrill of victory. Because as the hunter, he believed it was his responsibility to cause as little harm as possible. Because he felt he had betrayed the animal.

He was determined to come back, to find the wounded elk later and take it, but we were losing light fast and wouldn't have time to clean the kill anyway. We needed to find the trail soon. He told me he'd killed twenty-one elk in twenty-two years and had never, not once, lost an animal. I couldn't help but feel like a bad luck charm. Exhausted and dejected, we walked away from the hunt.

In our erratic wandering after the trail of blood, like dogs, we'd ended up far from where we started and far from where we needed to be, tucked on a side slope near the back of the canyon we'd hiked up and around earlier. Our path out was a rocky chute, covered with crumbling boulders, and even that would only put us back on the trail, where we'd have another few miles to go until we made it back to the car. I was cold now as the sun began to set, and my thighs quivered with exertion. My knees ached from the sheer inclines up and down. My legs felt so heavy I could barely keep moving, but we had no choice. Crab-walking up and over rocks, ankles wobbling, slipping, scraping my hands on bare rock, I kept going.

LATER, IN MY motel room, exhaustion overtook me as I peeled the sweaty clothes off my body, shedding stained base layers like dead skin, setting my heavy wet boots on a plastic bag to catch the mud that would harden and flake off in the night. My whole body trembled as I slowly let down my hair, and even that was painful. I sank down into the hot water filling the shallow motel tub, letting my knees poke up over the surface, soaking nearly into sleep, the water relaxing the soreness even from my scalp. I climbed into dry clothes and a deep slumber.

The next morning, I wandered around Missoula like a hunchback, my quadriceps quivering with the exertion of the hike, my hip flexors tight and unrelenting. My knee joints pulsed with radiating soreness, but I smiled a little at this. As much pain as I was in, I knew that I'd handled it, that I hurt because I had hunted. Gradually, over the course of the morning, and my flight back to Iowa, my muscles loosened. The tension released its grip, and I walked fully upright.

The night before our hunt, when I'd met Rick for drinks at the restaurant where he'd been with a group of other people, we told the story of the hunt we had planned. Another writer there laughed and said, "This is your first time hunting and you're starting with elk? That's like learning to fly-fish with steelhead!" I laughed along with him, though I didn't catch the reference.

But later, I spoke quietly to the fisherman and he told me about how sacred fishing was to him. He said, "You stay focused on that animal. Sometimes there will be other people around and it won't feel right—but when I'm about to take a fish, I look right down at the water and focus all my attention there and put on the blinders and block everything else out. That's when everything slows down and fades away. And all the little things, like tying a knot and casting the perfect line, become important. No matter how many people are around, it is a liturgy."

"And those little actions," I said, "are your prayers."

ON THE DAY of the hunt, by the time we made it back to the car, it had been dark for hours. It wasn't until I sat down that I realized how freezing cold I was, feet soaking wet in the puddles inside my boots, muscles vibrating in sheer exhaustion, nothing left to give but warnings. I was done moving for the day. The drive back faded in and out of memory. Rick fed me chewable aspirin for my knees but didn't take any for himself, saying his discomfort was on autopilot. Our headlights cut around the swerving mountain road out of the canyon and we spoke only in scraps.

"One thing I'll remember," I told him, "is how little advantage it turns out a gun is."

After hours of hiking, walking carefully through woods, avoiding branch-snapping or rock-knocking, he got one shot off, one time, and missed from seventy yards away. The gun was the only chance he ever had at taking an animal, and that had surprised me.

And he told me this wasn't how most people hunted. Mostly, he said, people get up before dawn and hike in while the elk are out for their morning feed. They camp out, in a tree or lying down, load their guns, and wait. They wait for the full, tired elk to return to their beds for the day, unaware, and they fire at them. That, he told me, was a lot easier.

I laughed a little. I couldn't imagine such a thing as easy right now.

"Yeah," he said, "it's a fuckin' hard way to get meat."

Chapter Fifteen

From Scratch

PULLED INTO MY new driveway in Kansas in the hot, whipping winds of an August thunderstorm, the sky a light gray streaked with darkness, rain barely falling but stinging sideways. I stepped into an empty living room, into my new house, alone in one of the last places I could have ever imagined living, and thought, *Okay. Now I get to build something.*

When I moved to Iowa for graduate school, I had a pretty serious existential crisis. My early twenties had been spent moving frequently, hopping across the country with stops in a city, a ski resort town, a seaside surf paradise, and my old college haunt. By the time I packed up the U-Haul again for Iowa, I began to feel ready to settle down in one place. But the Midwest had never been the place I imagined myself. Here I was, moving again, just when I was beginning to get sick of it, headed straight for a place I had little interest in calling home.

In 2011, years had passed since that move, and much to my surprise, I'd fallen in love with the Midwest, and could see myself making a home and a life there. The last thing I pictured myself as, when I left California, was a meat-eating feminist in the Great Plains. I've learned to never say never—and that the differences that separate one person from another, one region from the next, are far less important than the forces that connect us. What I discovered in the Midwest was that finding commonality was more about how than where. You had to choose the place you wanted to call home.

Throughout the winter of my last year in Iowa, as the reality of impending graduation slowly sank in, I realized I was going to have to find a job. The need was urgent: my new student loans and my old ones in deferment were going to need to be paid, and my three-year respite from the rest of the country's recession was up. Scott and I had split up, the pressure and complexity of planning a future together too much to handle. I was ready to set out on my own.

The job market wasn't easy, even with a graduate degree and thesis. By May, I had completed more than one hundred applications and two interviews, but had no offers. In July 2011, when the offer came, it was for a teaching job in a small town in rural western Kansas, a town with no co-op, no CSA shares, but plenty of dusty, open land.

AFTER I'D UNPACKED and returned the U-Haul truck, I kicked a path through the boxes lining the walls of my new apartment. The very first place I visited was the grocery store, where I very quickly learned that things were going to be different in Kansas. The one store in town, a regional chain grocery, showed me what I had suspected but hoped against: I had been spoiled to spend the last three years in a town with a large grocery co-op, an à la carte CSA, a meat and seafood buying club, and a year-round farmers market. As I began weaving through the aisles in the Kansas grocery store, searching for free-range eggs, specialty cheese, even national chain organic brands, I realized just how spoiled.

The produce section offered a small organic subset, where I picked up bell peppers, a bunch of kale, a pint of cherry tomatoes, and some seedless green grapes. All were from California, and I knew they would rot quickly, even in my refrigerator, after their long transport. Standing in the tiny section, I began to realize why so many people think organic is frivolous, a luxury for the wealthy elite. Two seemingly identical bags of green grapes sat side by side, one priced at $0.99 a pound, the other at $3.99 a pound. Even I had a hard time justifying the extra spending. I was on a tight budget and knew that there wasn't enough organic produce for me to avoid buying conventional. If it's not all organic, does it matter if anything is?

Near the produce section, a small corner of the store was marked off as "Nature's Market," denoted by a handwritten sign on a piece of neon-orange poster board, where I found some familiar foods: Muir Glen organic tomato sauce, Kashi cereal, Annie and her little bunnies on the macaroni and cheese. I hushed the voice in my head reminding me that many of these were corporate subsidiary brands and focused on the absence of high fructose corn syrup. I tossed a can of wild-caught albacore tuna and a few cans of refried beans into my cart and that was it. The end of the natural section.

I stared into the refrigerator section, trying to spot my egg and dairy options. The store's national organic brand, something called "Naturally Preferred," was my only option for milk, eggs, and yogurt. No longer did I have the choice between industrial-organic Horizon and Iowa-local Picket Fence. I had to hope that this industrial dairy raised their animals somewhat sustainably, because it was Naturally Preferred or conventional dairy and eggs from caged hens.

Standing in front of the freezer section, I wondered what kind of a sea change had struck the country in the two years since I'd stopped being a vegetarian. I saw a plethora of meat substitute products: MorningStar, Boca, Quorn of all colors; three different brands of tofu; seitan, tempeh, and even Yves fake lunch meats. But no actual meat.

My new grocery store had nothing in the way of free-range, antibiotic-free, humanely slaughtered meat.

Standing next to the weekly coupon flyer and just down from the ham-wrapped chicken breasts, packed by the dozen, I thought, *No wonder people think it's pointless to be a vegetarian. No wonder no one knows why chemically processed food is bad for us.* No longer were the notions that Americans drink too much sugar and eat too little produce abstractions for me. They were realities, ones I saw in my own shopping cart, with a paltry bunch of kale buried under boxes and cans and plastic.

I'd assumed that, since the remarkable foodscape in Iowa was a result of the plethora of farms there, and since Kansas was dotted with farmland, agriculture in Kansas would be the same: verdant fields brimming with produce, markets overflowing with a variety of sustainable, biodynamic, local options.

It was a thoroughly depressing trip to the grocery store but an educational one. Finally, I was going to have to live in a more modest food world, building a healthy diet from scratch, from the table scraps many Americans have to choose from. I would have to go outside the boundaries of the existing system and find the new one, work harder, spend more, drive farther to find the food I believed in eating.

I'D BEEN AN intellectual, an activist, and a vegetarian for large parts of my adult life, so I'd gotten used to people's misperception that I thought of myself as somehow their moral superior. My friend Liz described the sensation as being labeled "that" person—the troublemaker. The one who wants to know whether the T-shirts for the fundraiser at work are slave-free, whether the chocolate is rainforest certified.

An old college acquaintance named Bob was one of a handful of people to tell me that I was kind of a snob for being a vegetarian. Once, on a road trip back to college from New Jersey, some friends and I stopped at a McDonald's to grab dinner. As I scanned the menu for the scant vegetarian options I knew must be there somewhere, in the form of a grilled cheese or a baked potato, I listened to my friends order milkshakes, McRibs, double cheeseburgers, fries.

When my turn came to order, I sighed a little in frustration and told the cashier, "Just a side salad, please."

Bob scoffed, barely attempting to hide it beneath his breath, and rolled his eyes at me. "You think you're better than us. You think you're too good for this stuff, don't you?"

I shrugged Bob off then, but the short answer was—yes. Even though I was willing to eat a large McDonald's fries for dinner, yes I did. And that was part of the problem.

When I was a vegetarian, my idea of eating ethically was binary: there were right options and wrong ones, good and bad. In setting myself apart from the food system by boycotting meat, I looked away from the true complexity of the situation. Sure, sometimes people eat junk food because they like it, but when people rely on fast food or convenience store produce, it's because they are without other options. They do it because it's right next door. They do it because they can get a whole meal for the five bucks left in their wallets. They do it on road trips, when there are no kitchens or grocery stores, when there's no time to sit down. They do it because they've got only five minutes to eat before they have to change uniforms and get to their second job. They do it because it's the cheapest, the fastest, the closest. I was one of the lucky few who could afford to decide I was too good for that choice.

Buying back into our existing food system by eating meat again was a step towards owning up to the contradiction and naïveté of that past self. I wanted to participate in changing the food system because I wanted everyone to have the same options I know I've been lucky to have my whole life—the option to buy the best possible food, and to buy it close to home, for an affordable price. The know-how and the time to cook it so that it tastes amazing and is healthy. I wasn't naïve enough to think that was the world we live in. I understood that people who think of vegetarians or locavores or patrons of Whole Foods as elitist snobs think that way because in this world, organic, local vegetables are more expensive and harder to come by.

And so I was no longer angry at people who misunderstood sustainable eating; I knew that it was incredibly privileged. Instead, I was angry at the system. I was angry at the absence of grocery stores, or the absence of fresh food in convenience stores. I was angry at the proliferation of fast food. I was angry at the system that prevented low-income minorities from having the choice to buy fresh vegetables instead of a bacon cheeseburger.

I wanted a system that allowed anyone the option to buy organic, one that allowed anyone who wanted to eat meat a safe and humane way to get it. I wanted a system in which we all knew where our food came from, what it took to grow it, and how to cook it when we got home. I wanted a system in which the good food cost less and where we all had a little more time to spend in the kitchen, with our families.

I wanted a world in which everyone, even if they lived in food deserts like Southeast D.C. or West Oakland, California, or Rogers Park, Chicago, could walk a few blocks and buy something fresh and local. I wanted everyone to have a community they could learn through food, an access point to the natural landscape somewhere just outside the city, a means to understanding the rotating cycle of the season. Food is the fiber of our bodies, of our children's bodies, the pillar of our health. This was the same lesson Nona was teaching us when she made the whole family cram around the dining room table, even if it meant dragging folding chairs out of the closet and bumping elbows as we passed the lasagna. Food is where a community comes together. And no one should be left out of that landscape because of where they live, how much they make, or what color skin they have.

BUT I WASN'T perfect, even now, even still. My diet now was a series of small trade-offs, ones I was constantly making between practicality, availability, budget, and ideals. I couldn't visit every farm for every ingredient, but I knew a tomato that came off the vine today would always taste better than one that travelled cross-country in the back of a freezer truck. I didn't buy exclusively organic, but I knew how to use my salad spinner. I still ate comfort food, but I baked my own macaroni and cheese now. Sometimes, I just wanted a Dorito. I didn't have all the answers. But I was committed to asking the questions.

In Kansas, I was ready to do the work: to move beyond throwing my hands up or boycotting out of frustration. To let go of the black and white, and find a way to live in the messy gray that most of us occupy most of the time.

The Wednesday after my disappointing trip to the grocery store, I drove over to the weekly Hays Area Farmers Market, expectations appropriately low. It didn't look like much at first. From the stoplight on Vine Street, I could see the signs, but from this vantage point, the market seemed to me to be a handful of cars with their trunks open in a dirt wallow. But when I turned down 22nd Street to find a place to park, I was floored by the sheer amount of traffic. Lines of cars flowed in and out of the market's parking lot, and the one adjacent to it. From here, I could see about ten vendors, some of whom were selling out of their trunks.

I got out of the car feeling a well of hope but self-conscious, as I always am whenever I'm in a new place somewhere in the middle of the country, afraid that I'll be read immediately as a city-dwelling outsider, my dark sunglasses and skinny jeans met with incredulous stares. But slowly, I began to thaw. I kicked myself more than once for having bought something at the store that it turned out I could have gotten here, for thinking garlic would be too specialized an ingredient to hope for at so small a market, for not anticipating that potatoes would still be in season. In this way, the Hays market reminded me of one of the great joys of finding local produce—it teaches you something new about the place you live. Learning I could get russet potatoes in August in Kansas reminded me that I lived in a new climate now, one called the High Plains, with hints of subtropics and desert, a completely unique place with no parallel in North America. A place with its own identity.

I left the farmers market that day with summer squash, cucumber, sweet onions, and Sun Gold tomatoes, and a lot more on the wish list for next time, including homemade preserves, salsa and apple butter, okra, potatoes, watermelon, cantaloupe, and a whole lot of seriously delicious-looking baked goods sold by women wearing bonnets.

FOOD CONNECTS US to each other, and when we begin the process of weaving individual lives together, we create the elaborate tapestry known as community. Where food meets people, it's easy to put your finger on the essence of a place. Every farmers market I've ever shopped at has had its own distinct character, a flurry of booths and bartering, a sensory experience defined by the place, brought to life in a new urban-pastoral tableau.

Some places I've lived didn't have much of a market—like Bozeman, whose weekly Bogert Park market abutted the summer sounds of kids swimming in the adjacent municipal pool. I'd head there from work on a Tuesday evening and wander aimlessly with a cloth bag beneath the park's arching concrete shelter, often picking up only a few herbs or a loaf of bread, the booths occupied more by craftspeople than farmers, because Montana is mostly cattle and wheat country. I bought jewelry and soy candles there, petted shelter dogs up for adoption and goats on display next to their cheese maker. But there was always live bluegrass music, an irreplaceable component of a Montana summer. Sometimes I'd pack a bottle of wine and a blanket, buy some bread and cheese, and sit and watch small children swing in circles with their parents to the foot-stomping rhythm of the upright bass.

Although a market illuminates the seasonality of the produce, and therefore the climate of a place, it embodies more than that, too, by teaching us something about the character of the people who live there. The Ames market is held at the old train depot, a testament to the transcontinental railroad on whose back the town was built. The Bedford, New Hampshire, market, where my parents shop now, has a police officer on duty to direct traffic in and out of the gravel parking lot dotted with Lexuses and Audis. In these details, we learn who our neighbors are. For this reason, for the people, my favorite market by far is the one in Ithaca, New York.

A massive open-air wood pavilion, built specifically for the market, sits on the dock landing of Cayuga Lake, where the first Native American trading posts once were, bustling with nearly 150 vendors selling everything from rhubarb to handwoven black ash baskets to crepes and Vietnamese food. The Ithaca market has it all: vibrant produce grown by a swath of dedicated back-to-the-landers who drive their biodiesel vans down from the eco-village intentional community to stuff bunches of carrots or heads of radicchio into cloth bags; hippie artisans sporting dreadlocks or tattooed arms, sewing hammocks from hemp or making their own lavender soap; new urbanite entrepreneurs, giving free samples of their latest Pinot Noir; and a variety of food vendors that speak to the city's mixed cultural heritage: Tibetan, Mexican, Sri Lankan, Cuban. I've ridden the two miles to the market on my bike from my purple rental house by the gorge and been unable to find a spot to lock up, so crowded were the many racks the city provided there.

I love the Ithaca market as much as I do not because it's the best market, or has the most to offer, but because it's the most perfect illustration of what Ithaca is, this wild, chaotic city of ex-hippies and young professionals, stuffed to the brim with Tibetan monks protesting on the Commons, Christian communes running yerba maté shops, and poets hosting slams on

Friday nights. And the Ithaca market manages, somehow, with art and nature and food, to communicate all that.

Farmers markets connect us directly to the place we live—both in terms of people and food. We learn what the soil of our own backyards is capable of growing and when. But we also learn who are neighbors are and what kind of music they like, we learn what age they tend to be, what they wear, and how committed they are to our shared place. And learning all that is the first step to placing ourselves within that giant quilt, the beginning of finding our own identity within the fabric of a place.

SLOWLY, INTO THE autumn and winter in Kansas, a small network began to emerge, like a map for navigating my new town. A colleague pointed me towards a natural foods store I hadn't found even in my Googling, in a town still developing its Internet presence, out of its rural roots and into the digital age, where I found my natural body care products, herbal teas, and free-range bison meat from Wyoming. Finding food in Kansas, then, wasn't all smooth and easy. The search took more effort than filling out an online order form for wild-caught Alaskan salmon or stopping at the co-op on the way home from school. But maybe that's an opportunity to learn more, to spend more time meeting the people I was buying from, to help build and create the networks to transform this town, a sustainable food possibility waiting to happen.

During my first semester teaching on my new campus, the dean of my college asked, knowing a little about my background and writing interests, if I'd consider joining the university sustainability initiative. At the year's first meeting, a bear of a physics professor, with small glasses and a trim beard, introduced himself to me as Tiny.

When he heard my name, he said, "Oh, yeah, the sustainable food girl, right?" And then he smiled cleverly and said, "Do you need an egg guy?"

Tiny, it turned out, raised hens in his backyard, because he was tired of the limited egg options at the grocery store. He wasn't looking to turn a profit, just cover feed costs. He was happy to provide me with eggs whenever I needed any, and I was welcome to come by and meet the hens, too. Tiny just asked that I donate a dollar or two per dozen and return the cartons for reuse.

A year and a half earlier, when I had watched the slaughter at Black Earth Meats, I'd felt a little stunned, confused even, by where this journey had taken me. Along the path to find a truly mindful, sustainable way to eat, I'd seen so much more than I expected. I'd hiked in the woods of Montana behind a man with a rifle, and I'd crawled on my knees through the dirt, pulling turnips from the soil. I'd wandered wherever the search for ethical meat took me, into grazing pastures and henhouses and local butchers, and I'd been far outside my comfort zone. I knew I needed to see as much as I could, learn as much as I could, and I chased that idea down, trusting that, somehow, the way to eat meat ethically would reveal itself to me.

The next week, bringing a couple of wrinkled dollar bills to Tiny at a faculty meeting, I couldn't help but feel I was on the other side of something. I'd done the dramatic. I'd seen the shocking. I was scaling back down from the deep investigation that it took to understand the complexities of being a modern American omnivore, and now I had to find a way to weave these discoveries into my daily life. Now, being an ethical eater meant a careful daily practice.

I reminded myself that activism is about action. I knew sometimes the steps I took would seem small compared to the complete change our food system needs. I knew I would sometimes find myself asking what difference it made, buying one carton of eggs from a neighbor, instead of from an industrial egg farm?

But I also knew, from all I'd seen in the two years since I'd started eating meat again, that I couldn't let the size and scope of the problem deter me from taking these small steps. I remembered the focused attention of the fly-fisher in Montana, his prayer to the fish whose life he was about to take. I remembered that seemingly small daily actions meant something. I knew I'd always carry the delicate dance of the slaughter in my memory, and that it would drive me forward, when those little actions seemed insignificant. I wanted to remember that real change comes slowly. Those small steps would add up to something, to a lasting sustainable life.

When I brought home my first recycled carton full of Tiny's backyard eggs, I saw what lasting change looked like. The subtleties of the shift might not always be apparent; this single carton of eggs might not change the world. But making these choices, living this way, would change me. I'd learned how to see food as devotion, and I knew that making the sometimes harder, more ethical choices would be a constant source of renewal and reward. Because when I looked at those eggs, I saw the landscape of truly local, communal food. Those eggs looked imperfect by the standards of any mega-chain grocery store, but they were beautiful to me: all varied sizes, speckled and brown, warm to the touch.

Epilogue

Making Meatballs

I **WAS ONLY IN** Kansas for a year. In the spring of 2012, I got a tenure-track job offer from a regional branch campus of the University of Pittsburgh. I packed up my Subaru again, this time with a dog as a companion, and drove myself across the country to the small postindustrial city of Johnstown, Pennsylvania.

This is where I've finally found a sense of stability in a secure job and a community of writers, with a nearby city that provides a rich cultural landscape. This is also where I fell in love and got married. This is where I turned thirty, and where, finally, I began to feel settled.

Johnstown is a city still ravaged by the departure of its steel mills, a place heavy with poverty and the resultant problems of crime and addiction, a city of chain grocery stores and a population without much disposable income. But it's also a city with five neighborhood farmers markets during the warm months. In Pennsylvania, I've found neither an easy food paradise like

Iowa nor a food desert, but a middle ground: local and organic is still more expensive, but it's available and becoming more common.

I'm still an omnivore, and I still struggle often with the choices I make. I sometimes succumb to the allure of junk food, the convenience of processed food, the ease of ignoring a conventional label. When I find myself starting to feel overwhelmed by choice and sacrifice, I try to return to the principle of connection: if I can't eat perfectly, I want to try to eat with as much mindfulness of my part in the web as possible.

I try to remember Montana, the night before I went hunting, when I spoke to the fly-fisher about why I was there. When I told him my story, he told me he thought catching and eating meat the ethical, sustainable way was more honest and more morally correct than being a vegetarian. He said people who thought vegetarianism was the solution were willingly putting on blinders—just like I did when I tried to ignore the corporate connections behind my Boca Burger. Unless you never drive a car, he said, never buy a foreign-made article of clothing, never use chemically produced body products, you are causing suffering, too.

"We all kill a little," he said. "The least you can do is look at it."

WHAT I'VE SEEN of living animals on real small farms, and what I've learned about corporate connections, environmental degradation, and human suffering in the food system suggests to me that the way an animal is raised and killed for food—and, therefore, the choices I make about which animals to consume—is implicated in much more than a single meal. How the animal is raised impacts the ground on which it lives, the soil and the water and the air. The quality of that land impacts the farm and the farmer, environmentally and economically. The practices on a farm and the pricing of food affect whether a community has enough jobs, which affects whether a person will be able to afford to eat. Whether someone buys that animal to eat affects how much the farmworkers get paid and their labor conditions. Eating an animal raised sustainably can have a serious positive influence on the eater's health, preventing them from eating processed food, toxic chemicals, high fructose corn syrup. Raising an animal the right way can sustain the earth's life; eating an animal raised the right way can sustain an individual's life.

For some people, the question of whether to eat meat will always be a purely animal rights issue, and I can respect that. That's where this story started for me, too. But now, I can't help but see the same question as an environmental issue; a labor rights issue; a fair trade issue; an issue of our global community's economic, environmental and human progress. If my goal is to live in harmony with my world, eating a hamburger doesn't have to run counter to those ideals. It can be a way to invest in them, to practice them every day, with every bite I take.

FOOD HAS BROUGHT me into connection with almost everyone I've ever met. You get someone talking about food, and they'll always have something to say. When I stayed on the farm in Wisconsin, Jenny took me for a girls' night out at the local bar. I spent hours talking with women who were otherwise strangers to me—potters and farmers and therapists—all of whom had food stories. One told me she'd been a vegetarian on and off most of her life because she'd grown up in eastern Colorado, downwind of the cattle feedlots. At a writer's conference in 2010, my roommate and I bonded over dinner as she taught me the nutritional values of cactus. I've heard stories of mushroom hunting and fly-fishing and raw foods–dieting. We all have something in common in the kitchen.

We don't have to have the same story—the point of connection is that we all have a story. Food gives us common ground, a subject of conversation, yes, but also the foundation for friendship, the sharing of values. It's taken me years to see, but I understand now that identity and community can coexist, that our values can be welcomed into the community we want to inhabit, that all of us have an individual responsibility to shape the world we want to live in, rather than to simply swear off it.

And ultimately, of course, changing the way I think about food led me back to my family. When I started eating meat again, I had no idea how to cook it. I was a complete beginner, which meant I got to start from scratch, to learn everything anew. It was natural—I didn't even notice myself doing it—to reach out to my family. When I went home for visits, I asked my mother to share her favorite recipes with me. I called my little sister, by now a world-class pastry chef and graduate of culinary school, to ask her about internal temperatures for steaks and pork chops. And eventually, I found myself returning to those old family recipes, remaking them my own.

Just a few months ago, I woke up to a rainy Sunday when I didn't have much to do and decided I wanted to spend the day cooking. I called my mom and got Nona's recipe for meatballs. I started on a pot of sauce, putting the tomato paste and puree over a low simmer, and gradually adding garlic and red pepper, basil and oregano, tasting as I went. I mixed together ground chuck and ground pork, sprinkled in paprika and parsley, a little egg and Parmesan cheese. And when I dug my hands into that sticky ground meat, I understood what it meant to be part of something, to be part of my family's lineage of backyard gardens and wine-stained kitchen tables. I felt connection, and I understood it had been there, waiting for me, all along. This was where I belonged.

Acknowledgments

THE FIRST AND greatest thanks go to my family, for all the ways in which they both literally and figuratively fed this book. Mom and Dad, I would be a completely different person without the unending support and encouragement you've offered my writing, from age five on. Thanks to you both, and to Meaghan and Caitlin, Nana and Gampi, and Uncle Paul, for sharing those first kitchens with me, and for continuing to cook together whenever we can.

Many thanks to the editors of the publications where excerpts from this book have previously appeared: "Slaughter-house" in *Alimentum*, "Gursha" in *The Inquisitive Eater*, "Catch & Release," in *Guernica*, "Garbanzo Beans for Breakfast" in *Fringe*, and "Elk Country" in *Creative Nonfiction*. Special thanks to Hattie Fletcher, whose keen editing on the last essay echoed through the entire manuscript.

I'm so happy to be a part of the Greystone Books family, and my endless thanks to everyone on the team who helped turn this manuscript into a real book. Special thanks to my editor, Jen Croll, for her enthusiasm and insight; to Rob Sanders for his welcoming and encouragement and to Shirarose Wilensky for her meticulous eye.

THE VEGETARIAN'S GUIDE TO EATING MEAT

Listing everyone that read or offered feedback on this book over its life-span would be almost impossible, but a few amazing teachers and friends were invaluable to its development. Thanks to the Bread Loaf Writer's Conference, my workshop crew there, and especially to Marytza K. Rubio, an unstoppable force of love and support. Thanks to my colleagues in the Humanities Division at Pitt-Johnstown, especially Michael Cox and Eric Schwerer, for guidance and solidarity while I tried to figure out how to teach full time and still finish this book.

Thanks to Sheila Squillante, Sheryl St. Germain, and Sherrie Flick for being wonder-woman role models. Thanks to Dave Housley, Mike Ingram, and Tom McAllister for always inviting me along and making me laugh. You're all the definition of good literary citizens. Each one of you has, at some point, given me the boost I needed to keep going.

I owe so much to the entire MFA program at Iowa State University, especially to my workshop cohort for being my earliest readers. Thanks to Scott Ricketts for being the first one to suggest this may be a book. Deb Marquart, Rachel Lopez, Liz Clift, and Rachael Button saw these pages when they were barely anything, believed in them, and helped me figure out what I was really trying to say.

I can never do enough to thank my two guiding lights: Dean Bakopoulos and Benjamin Percy. Dean, thank you for fresh eyes when I needed them most, for the potential you saw with them, and for pushing me to dig deeper. Ben, you saw this thing from beginning to end, and never let up. Thank you for always demanding that I work harder, risk more, and put three things in every list. This book wouldn't be this book without you.

So many farmers, hunters, gardeners, and chefs let me share their food while working on this book, but I owe a debt of gratitude to a few who opened their doors to me beyond what any reasonable person might expect. Thanks to Bartlett Durand for inviting me onto the slaughterhouse floor of Black Earth Meats. I can't wait to see what you do next. To Rink and Jenny, thank you for being so welcoming to a clueless suburbanite who had no idea how to cut arugula, and for offering me the little yellow house as a home for a few weeks. Highest thanks to Rick Bass, for taking a walk with me. I know how much I was asking, and I'm so grateful you were willing to let me join you.

Thanks to Bonnie and Becky, for embracing me as part of your family, and the gift of Thanksgiving on the farm.

Finally, thanks to my husband, Jeremy Justus, who also believes in showing his love through food. You're my favorite chef, the funniest person I know, and the greatest partner I could have imagined. I can't believe how lucky I am to share all of this with you.

Notes

Chapter Three

1. "Sodexo, the food services industry giant..." All Sodexo information from the Clean Up Sodexo advocacy campaign run by the Service Employees International Union: cleanupsodexo.org.

Chapter Four

1. "In a video piece released the next year, the Borf Brigade..." Borf Brigade, "Borf Brigade Communique," Online video clip, YouTube, August 21, 2006, accessed June 1, 2016.

2. "The Southeast quadrant of D.C... had a population that was more than 90 percent African American..." D.C. Hunger Solutions and Social Compact, "When Healthy Food Is out of Reach: Examining the Grocery Gap in the District of Columbia, 2010." www.dchunger.org/pdf/grocerygap.pdf.

3. "D.C. has the highest concentration of Ethiopians anywhere in the United States," BBC News, "Little Ethiopia: African Diaspora Who Call US Capital Home," BBC News, June 12, 2013, accessed June 1, 2016, www.bbc.com/news/magazine-22803973.

Chapter Five

1. "...a teenager in the next town over shot and killed the first legally hunted bison..." Scott McMillion, "Belgrade Hunter Bags Bison," *Bozeman Daily Chronicle*, November 15, 2005, www.bozemandailychronicle.com/news/article_8ba8f7b4-b1f1-5b40-b3b6-55f9b6b840ed.html.

2. "...bison nearly died off in the nineteenth century..." Historical information on bison hunts in this chapter is gathered from William T. Hornaday's *The Extermination of the American Bison*, Smithsonian Institution Press, 2000.

3. "General William Tecumseh Sherman..." All information in this paragraph about the U.S. military's support of bison slaughter as a means of eradicating indigenous populations comes from David D. Smits's article "The Frontier Army and the Destruction of the Buffalo: 1865–1883," *Western Historical Quarterly*, Vol. 25, No. 3, Autumn 1994, accessed September 16, 2016. history.msu.edu/hst321/files/2010/07/smits-on-bison.pdf.

4. "The Turner bison herd is nearly five thousand strong..." Paul Larmer, "Ted Turner: A Good Guy After All?" *High Country News*, July 17, 2013, accessed June 1, 2016, www.hcn.org/articles/ted-turner-conservationist-entrepreneur.

5. "Michael Perry has written that the land..." The original quote is "The land takes you back. All you have to do is show up. Finding your place among the *people*, now, that's a different proposition." *Population 485: Meeting Your Neighbors One Siren at a Time* (New York: Harper Perennial, 2002), 111.

Chapter Six

1. "Mati Waiya...the first Native American to hold a position as part of the Waterkeeper Alliance..." More information on Waiya, the Ventura Coastkeeper, and the International Waterkeeper Alliance can be found at the Wishtoyo Chumash Foundation's website: www.wishtoyo.org/new-page-62.

2. "...an investigative piece by journalist Eric Schlosser..." Eric Schlosser, "In the Strawberry Fields," *The Atlantic*, November 1995 issue, accessed June 1, 2016, www.theatlantic.com/magazine/archive/1995/11/in-the-strawberry-fields/305754.

3. "California had been the country's number one food and agricultural producer..." All statistics in this chapter on California's agricultural production come from a California State Senate Republican Caucus Briefing Report: "Our Agricultural Bounty—The True California Gold Rush," February 4, 2009, accessed April 1, 2011, cssrc.us/publications.aspx?id=5403&AspxAutoDetectCookieSupport=1.

4. "According to the California Institute..." All information in this chapter on migrant farmworkers' wages, health, and living conditions is garnered from a 2007 fact sheet presented by the North Carolina Farmworker Institute titled "United States Farmworker Factsheet," www.saf-unite.org/pdfs/ SAF%20Fact%20Sheet%20US07.pdf.

5. "California Food Policy Advocates estimates..." M. Pia Chaparro, Brent Langellier, Kerry Birnbach, Matthew Sharp, and Gail Harrison, "Nearly Four Million Californians Are Food Insecure," UCLA Center for Health Policy Research/California Food Policy Advocates, June 2012, accessed June 1, 2016, healthpolicy.ucla.edu/publications/Documents/PDF/FoodPBrevised7-11-12.pdf.

Chapter Eight

1. "Sometime that summer, a friend showed me a chart..." This chart was made by Phil Howard, an assistant professor of Community, Agriculture, and Recreation and Resource Studies at Michigan State University, for *GOOD* magazine. It appeared in the March/April 2008 issue of *GOOD* and can be viewed online here: awesome.good.is/features/009/009buyingorganic.html.

2. "... in 2001, a U.S. jury ordered Philip Morris..." "US Smoker Wins Billions in Damages," BBC World News, June 7, 2001, news.bbc.co.uk/2/hi/americas/1374451.stm.

3. "On appeal later that year, Philip Morris had the punitive damages reduced to $100 million..." "Judge Slashes Tobacco Award," *Guardian*, August 10, 2001, www.theguardian.com/uk/2001/aug/10/smoking.

4. "... raised 9 billion dollars..." Kathleen Pender, "Some Food for Thought on Philip Morris' $8 billion Kraft IPO/Analysts Mixed on Long-Term Prospects of Stock," *SF Gate*, June 12, 2001, articles.sfgate.com/2001-06-12/business/17601978_1_spin-off-of-kraft-foods-philip-morris-voting-rights.

5. "Tyson... paid more than $7.5 million in fines for twenty felony violations of the Clean Water Act..." Those fines came from a single Environmental Protection Agency investigation and litigation, the details of which can be found in this press release from the Department of Justice: www.justice.gov/archive/opa/pr/2003/June/03_enrd_383.htm.

Chapter Nine

1. "When I read Pollan's description of this visit..." Pollan writes extensively about Polyface Farms, but the first visit occurs on page 125 of *The Omnivore's Dilemma: A Natural History of Four Meals* (New York: Penguin, 2006).

   I want to be clear that I am not necessarily advocating for Joel Salatin as a model farmer but suggesting that Polyface was a beacon of hope in contrast to Pollan's frustration with industrial models of agriculture.

   For a critique of Salatin's framework of sustainable agriculture, in particular his articulation of free-market, anti-regulation politics and his focus on an overly white, masculine consumer base, see Ryanne Pilgeram and Russell Meeuf, "The Celebrity of Salatin: Can a Famous Lunatic Farmer Change the Food System?," *Journal of Critical Thought and Praxis*, Vol. 3: Iss. 1, Article 4, 2014, lib.dr.iastate.edu/jctp/vol3/iss1/4.

Chapter Eleven

1. "... Roger Cohen suggests that Americans..." Roger Cohen, "Advantage France," *New York Times*, August 30, 2009, accessed April 5, 2011, www.nytimes.com/2009/08/31/opinion/31iht-edcohen.html?_r=1&emc=eta1.

Chapter Fourteen

1. "The Native American tribes of the Great Plains..." The information in this chapter on the Plains tribes' bison hunting and dressing techniques comes from Steven Rinella's *American Buffalo: In Search of a Lost Icon* (New York: Spiegel & Grau, 2008).